Enneagram
Business

Create a Balance in Life Through the Enneagram

(A Guide Book Using Kundalini Yoga and the
Enneagram)

Joshua Maize

Published by Knowledge Icons

Joshua Maize

All Rights Reserved

Enneagram Business: Create a Balance in Life Through the Enneagram (A Guide Book Using Kundalini Yoga and the Enneagram)

ISBN 978-1-990084-54-6

Legal & Disclaimer

The information contained in this book is not designed to replace or take the place of any form of medicine or professional medical advice. The information in this book has been provided for educational and entertainment purposes only.

The information contained in this book has been compiled from sources deemed reliable, and it is accurate to the best of the Author's knowledge; however, the Author cannot guarantee its accuracy and validity and cannot be held liable for any errors or omissions. Changes are periodically made to this book. You must consult your doctor or get professional medical advice before using any of the

Table of Contents

Introduction

Enneagram is a typology machine that describes the human character as the number of interrelated character types. While it is popular within the spirituality and enterprise disciplines, there has been limited research on its use and is not largely routine in the subject of evidence-based psychology.

The enneagram consists of a nine-point diagram. Each factor represents a personality type. The enneagram figure or design is made up of three elements. The outer part is composed of a circle, which then incorporates a triangle and an irregular hexagon.

At its simplest, the Diagram represents 9 extraordinary character types. Beyond the simple 9 character types, the system grows a good deal more complex and includes 27 distinct subtypes, such as the

1

three major "centers" focused on action, emotion, and thinking.

Each type is demonstrated through a number of characteristics that dominate the general personality of the individual. This model additionally identifies the best fear of all types, as well as the coping mechanisms that humans use to deal with those concerns.

According to the Enneagram Institute, most anagram theorists believe that people are born with a dominant personality type that can then form with the help of environmental elements and experiences. These two forces also have a tendency to influence each other. Inborn characteristics and characteristics help in how humans react to their experiences, and the environment is a type of function in which character is constructed and expressed.

Chapter 1: Definition And Understanding

Of Enneagram

To begin with, the term Enneagram is a simple term which can be quite complicated in its understanding. However, with the help of this chapter, you will be able to create your definition on the concept. Being able to do so is essential in that it ensures that you understand the real meaning of Enneagram. The Enneagram can be defined as the study of human personalities, especially in their relationships or behaviors in a social setting. It is also a model for identification of who we actually are, and the nine personality types that are used in the analysis.

It is essential to know that because of how extensive the study is; it has different concepts aimed at different purposes but with a fundamental notion of "nine human personalities study." As a model, the Enneagram is understood to be a collection of interrelated personality types. Take for example, when you're around people, and you notice that some people are optimistic, happy and energetic, some are dull, or even in despair, some could be moving around aimlessly, while some remain quite still. Without knowing it, you have just conducted an enneagram study on those people.

As a typology of human personalities, Enneagram is referred to as the nine shades or sometimes called Enneatypes. This is indicated by a geometric figure known as enneagram points. It is the point where different personalities within a specified geometry meet with the reactions of different people at the same given scenario.

The growth of Enneagram has been tremendous and alarming at the spiritual and business levels as it had garnered momentum as regards these levels over the past few years. This is because they are the two significant social settings that deal with the co-existence of people for a relatively long time. The need to study Enneagram across the bounds of a specific geographical setting is pertinent. This is because even within two people, social relations can be established. Think about this, when you are in a conversation with someone, and suddenly their reaction dramatically changes - try to understand what caused this change.

In the long run, you will come to realize that everything boils down to your Enneagram. In other words, your personality and that of the other person's. It's little wonder why Enneagram is very important in our lives for a successful relationship with the people around us. These personalities are interwoven with yours, and they determine your relationships with people as well. In the line of business, Enneagram means the act of gaining more knowledge of how dynamic interpersonal thoughts affect diverse workers in their approaches to tasks at the workplaces. Interviewers use this Enneagram as a concept and a working mechanism in determining how the candidates will react to events surrounding them.

This will tell them the best candidates for their job. Instead of asking these workers about their job functions and responsibilities, Enneagram would focus more on the personalities of the workers as related to their line of duty. All of this is Enneagram at play. While in the spiritual setting, Enneagram is seen as what depicts a meaningful living and also an awareness of the state of living. Now the question we should ask ourselves is if this is all about Enneagram. This is how Enneagram operates spiritually in the real sense of the world. Be that as it may, we shouldn't forget that Enneagram is a broad concept with diverse settings and usage. Although they might seem to be an embodiment of these nine personality traits, they are also independent but interrelated. Furthermore, Enneagram is the best state or personalities believed to be true for all humans.

Additionally, the Enneagram is perceived as a personality system which combines nine different traits. Many accentuations have been made regarding the fact that humans have one of these personalities which consist of some subtypes as well. Well, you might wonder how these traits get to us; many people say we pick them up in childhood while other people say it is genetically related. Whatever your belief might be about these two assumptions, the fact that everyone behaves within specified traits in different ways remains true for every situation.

There are nine types of Enneagram generally. There are different attachments to these types, and they all have a placement within the symbol of the Enneagram. The nine personalities have different names, and they are as follows:

1. The Reformer,

2. The Helpers,

3. The Achievers,

4. The Individualist,

5. The Investigators,

6. The Loyalists,

7. The Enthusiasts,

8. The Challenger,

9. The Peacemakers.

In all the studies of Enneagram, one repeated and fascinating factor that has come up is that people within a given type of trait will be different from one another. The reason for this is yet to be ascertained, but it could be because humans are dynamic. In fact, everyone, including you, could be a challenger within a particular time and then change to an enthusiast some other times.

Many psychologists believe that every change in human traits premises on the state of mental health. Further opinions are still subject to researchers though. Healthiness or unhealthiness state is defined as what a particularly given quality finds pleasurable and natural to them against what they see and do as otherwise. The focus of this chapter is not to provide in-depth information about the personalities; it will be dealt with in the chapters to follow.

However, it is to open your mind and introduce you to the concept of Enneagram. That way, you will be able to understand the following chapters as you read them. There are different levels in the personalities' types which contribute to their healthiness as well. In order to explain Enneagram in total, there are separate wings created for them. These wings will be adequately discussed later in this book.

However, what they explain is the fact that many people have combinations of Enneagram personalities. Even though the nine personalities are true to humans, there are more combinations to these personalities than the existence of their singular presence. This makes postulation of rules that capture their behavior a mirage and vague.

It is pertinent to note that there are different names given to these personalities. This could be because they have different teachings, context, and usage of the information. Whatever angle enneagram studies might take in the future, one fact remains that it is a nine-personality study and a model to understanding the ways, actions, and reactions that occur in social relationships.

In conclusion, Enneagram encapsulates the system of the nine human personalities that determine the trait which signals why people react and act in the way they do. The people that developed it might have not even imagined it could be real Enneagram. This is because many people have altered the probability of having the Enneagram in its holistic nature. , but its reality is shown even in these non believers. This is the power of Enneagram.

Trust me -nothing is stopping you from becoming a better version of yourself - besides yourself. You are your own biggest rival and enemy towards achieving this fantastic trait. If only you can look past your weaknesses and emotions, understanding people's personalities would be at your fingertips. That way, you would be able to thrive in your workplace, relationships, and other social outings. The next chapter focuses on how Enneagram began as a concept, idea, and term. You don't want to miss it.

Chapter 2: The Enneagram Figure

The most intriguing part of the entire Enneagram personality test is the actual Enneagram figure. It has been so precisely developed that it resembles something that mathematicians would love to work with.

The figure has three main parts: a circle, an inner triangle, and an irregular hexagonal figure. Around the out circle are the numbers 1 to 9, which follow each other in regular order around the circle. Not only are these shapes essential for determining the right personality, but they also each have a kind of symbolic meaning about them.

For example, the circle represents unity and the circle of life. It is there to show you that everything has a beginning and an end, and that we are all part of a whole which connects us all. It is a beautiful reminder that everything we do in life is somehow connected to ourselves and to all the people around us. We would not be able to survive on our own if it wasn't for the help and support of the people who we know and of the nature that surrounds us and that we draw our energy primarily from.

The triangle in the middle of the circle represents the 'law of three'. This is one of the two essential patterns in the life of human beings. It is the pattern of where the number three has a symbolical meaning to the way things happen. For example, if two good things have already happened to you in a single day, it is very likely that there will be a third event as well to complete the rule of three. This may not be a rule that people are quickly aware of often, but if you stop to meditate on its purpose for a moment, you will soon notice that the 'rule of three' is everywhere around you.

The final piece of the puzzle is the hexagon that represents the 'law of seven'.

Similarly to the 'law of three', this law is also deeply engraved in human mathematics and also in the nature that surrounds us. It is based on arithmetic laws, and has been a crucial development in the research of some of our greatest geniuses in history. Such as Nikola Tesla and Albert Einstein.

It is now likely much clearer why these specific symbols were used for the development of the Enneagram figure. It was not something that was just randomly created to satisfy a need. Rather, it is based on such strong facts and logic in our own being and the nature that surrounds us, that it is no wonder that the Enneagram can so accurately depict the personality of the human being.

Now that the basics of the Enneagram and its history have been covered, we can move on to the most exciting part of this journey, which is figuring out your own personality type and what it means for you and for your future growth.

One thing that must be stressed before we begin though is that it is crucial to truly follow all the steps of the Enneagram properly and to the best of your abilities. It is also very important that the search for your personality type must come at a time when you are truly feeling comfortable with yourself and with your emotions. This means that it is ill advised to complete this test at a time when you are too angry or even too happy, as well as at a time when you are tired or hungry, for example. If at all possible, choose a moment when you feel like you are truly yourself to the best of your own abilities, because this is when you will be able to make the most of this journey.

Likewise, some people have decided to take the test a number of times. Unfortunately, this does not work in the case of the Enneagram, because each time you take the test anew, you could be unconsciously working towards a result that you are hoping to get as opposed to the result that truly belongs to you. This is why you must never rush it. Relax, take your time, and be yourself. Make notes along the way if you need to, and make sure that no one is able to interrupt you until you reach the very end of the Enneagram.

How the Enneagram Works

Although the structure of the Enneagram looks complicated when you first look at it, as you become familiar with its functions and all of the things that you can achieve with it, it will soon become part of your daily life ritual and a deeper understand of who you are.

The best way to start the process is to actually sketch the Enneagram with your own hand. Simply look at a picture of the Enneagram, and then slowly recreate it onto a piece of paper. Do not rush this drawing. You really want to make sure that you pay attention to every stroke of your hand, and especially when all of the numbers are placed on the symbol. This is an important step because it will help you familiarize yourself with the Enneagram, and also because it will be easier to recall it back in your memory once you have recreated yourself at least once.

Also pay special attention to where each number lies on the symbol and how it is itself connected to the triangle and the hexagon within the circle (which we have mentioned before already). Do not write the numbers anywhere else that they are not supposed to be, and also do not draw the triangle or the hexagon in any other position other than the one that they were meant to be in. Although it is wonderful to encourage creativity in your life, this is not the right moment to do so because each part of the Enneagram symbol has a very specific place which it must occupy if it is to make sense and to bring you the personality results that you are expecting to receive.

Once you have completed the drawing once, go back and do it a few more times.

Ideally, you would want to do this as many times as it takes for you to learn how to draw the Enneagram entirely by heart. If possible, do not move forward in your journey until you have successfully completed this step.

Chapter 3: Origins And History Of The Enneagram

The history of the enneagram, also referred to as the enneagram of personality types, in modern society can be traced back to Oscar Ichazo and George Gurdjieff. In the early-mid 1900s, they described how everyone has a unique personality that they identify with within the enneagram. These personalities represent the way we behave, feel and think.

The ancient history of the enneagram is largely undocumented, but it is believed that the concept existed in the Middle East and Asia thousands of years ago. The issue of documentation arises because, during these times, the enneagram was more of a spoken tradition than a written discipline. It is through the works of Ichazo and Gurdjieff, and later on Claudio Naranjo in the 1970s, that the modern concept of the enneagram became popular.

Today many experts have built on this knowledge and presented their own concepts of determining personalities and self-discovery. Some of the terminology used by different experts overlap from one method to another.

Some of the earliest practitioners in the field claimed that their knowledge of the enneagram of personality types was as a result of their interaction with ancient traditions. Because of their inability to prove or authenticate their sources, historical construct of the enneagrams from their perspective has remained ambiguous and has since been largely discarded or disregarded.

George Gurdjieff spent most of his life learning about wisdom, religions, and the traditions that define them. He was an astute businessman, philosopher, and a very spiritual man. During his exploits, Gurdjieff became a teacher, imparting knowledge about human consciousness wherever he went.

According to Gurdjieff, most people do not live to fulfill their purpose in life because while they think they are living, they are actually asleep. He championed the idea that personality and essence are two different things. In his teachings, personalities are learned, which is why it is possible to mimic a personality. On the other hand, the essence is inborn.

Though Gurdjieff is often credited for his role in the development of the enneagram, he never took credit for it. However, he also barely acknowledged any sources. There are many theories about the source of his work, including his interaction with desert mothers and fathers or the Sufis. Some theorists also believe his work might be traced back to theories from ancient Greece.

Whatever the specific inspiration of his work was, the consensus is that most of the work Gurdjieff did towards the enneagram was a result of the interactions he had with people in different environments as he traveled the world.

Ichazo's work picked up from where Gurdjieff left off. His studies were largely influenced by Confucianism and Buddhism, alongside other spiritual affiliations he interacted with. Ichazo wrote several articles on enneagrams, in some of them refuting the earlier claims by Gurdjieff on the sources of his work. According to Ichazo, most of the teachings were picked up from ancient Greek philosophers, the Magi, and some Hindu scriptures. Therefore, it was his belief that Gurdjieff had no role to play in the enneagram, especially since the teachings he publicized were purely universal.

Ichazo then introduced a system which he referred to as protoanalysis, which refers to the methodologies he used in his teachings. In these teachings, Ichazo introduced more than 100 enneagrams.

Building on Ichazo's work came Dr. Claudio Naranjo. Naranjo's work from 1970 was influenced by tragedy when his son died on the eve of Easter. This tragedy forced him on a journey of spiritual discovery, which saw him seek Ichazo's help in Chile. Naranjo proceeded with his studies and discoveries in the field, writing lots of informative books about the enneagram. Since then, interest in enneagrams has grown, with many students trying to expound on the existing knowledge.

Some other notable contributors to the enneagram of personality types include David Daniels, Helen Palmer, Russ Hudson, Don Riso, Theodore Donson, and Kathy Hurley.

Chapter 4: The Theory Of Enneagram

No one is 100% certain where the Enneagram theory started. Some people believe it can be traced back mathematically, while others state it started through spirituality and Christianity. Plotinus, a Greek philosopher who lived in 200 A.D, spoke of nine principles of the human personality. Ramon Llull, a mathematician from the 13th century also spoke on nine personality types (Cloete, n.d.).

However, no matter how far back you trace the Enneagram theory, you will find an evolution devoted to it. Today, the Enneagram theory is a diagram which looks to identify a person's personality. However, many psychologists have also used this theory to identify people in large groups (Cloete, n.d.).

How it Works

One of the distinctive factors about the Enneagram theory is it doesn't put people into a box. Within the nine main types of personalities are 27 subtypes. On top of this, in each personality there are wings, lines, and other factors that help determine your unique personality (Cloete, n.d.). While the theory and diagram might seem complicated at first, as it is complex, it becomes easier to understand it the more you learn the details about the types, subtypes, and how the theory works in general.

Diagrams

The Enneagram Diagram

In order to help you understand the diagram of the Enneagram, you will want to look at it step by step. This will help you better understand and follow the basic structure of the Enneagram. For instance, you can start by looking at the diagram as a circle. Around this circle, you will see the numbers nine through one. While the numbers are numerical, if you go counter-clockwise, they are also placed in a systematic order, which is why nine is at the top. Each of these nine numbers represents a personality type, which you can identify in the diagram above.

People often get confused about the lines within the circle. As you can see, there are a variety of lines which go from one number to the next. These are the lines that guide you to your personality and your personality's wings. Again, if you take the lines one by one, you will gain a better understanding of the Enneagram.

First, take a look at numbers nine, six, and three. You will notice that when they are connected, they create an equilateral triangle. From there, you will want to look at the connections of numbers through six points which construct an irregular hexagram. You will want to make sure you follow the order below as the points have to be followed in this order.

number 1 connects to 4

number 4 connects to 2

number 2 connects to 8

number 8 connects to 5

number 5 connects to 7

number 7 connects to 1

When looking at the lines within the Enneagram, you will find that there are arrows which lead you to the following number.

9 Types + 27 Subtypes

You should never think that your personality will fall under just one type of personality. In fact, you will find pieces of your personality in all of the other personalities. However, you should also find the primary number associated with your personality. This number will represent the biggest part of your personality. Remember, the Enneagram is meant to take you out of a box, not put you into one. This is why your personality will be scattered throughout the diagram, but you will have one primary number.

In this section, I will run through the nine types and 27 subtypes that can form your personality. I will not go through these types and subtypes in detail within this section. Instead, the following chapters will be dedicated to each one of the nine types, where I will further discuss the types, subtypes, and other factors in detail.

The nine personality types of the Enneagram are as follows (Berkers, n.d.):

The Perfectionist

The Helper

The Achiever

The Individualist

The Investigator

The Loyalist

The Enthusiast

The Protector

The Mediator

There are a total of 27 subtypes within these nine personality types. There are three main categories that hold these subtypes. These categories are social, self-preservation, and one-on-one (Cloete, n.d.).

The social category focuses on how we get along with other people and our social instincts. It outlines how we maintain relationships and how we work with others. The social category also focuses on how we strive to do the best we can for other people (Cloete, n.d.).

The self-preservation category focuses on how well we preserve our body and mind. It relates to the ways we manage stress and other life events. It is the category that focuses on our emotions. This category looks at ways for us to do our best when it comes to preserving ourselves mentally, physically, and emotionally (Cloete, n.d.).

The one-on-one category focuses on the legacies we want to leave for future generations. Everyone, whether it is within your family or in the world, wants to be remembered when they leave this earth. This category focuses on how we take control of these types of situations. It further dives into our more personal one-on-one relationships with people and environmental factors. Through this category, we can determine what we want to leave behind and how we want to do our best while still on this earth (Cloete, n.d.).

Each personality type has one subtype within the social, self-preservation, and one-on-one category. To gain a better understanding of this, as it is complex, I will list each personality type with its category and subtype below. I will go into each subtype in detail later.

The Perfectionist

Social: Not adaptable

Self-preservation: Worry

One-on-one: Zeal

The Helper

Social: Ambition

Self-preservation: Privilege

One-on-one: Seduction

The Achiever

Social: Prestige

Self-preservation: Security

One-on-one: Charisma

The Individualist

Social: Shame

Self-preservation: Tenacity

One-on-one: Competition

The Investigator

Social: Totem

Self-preservation: Castle

One-on-one: Confident

The Loyalist

Social: Duty

Self-preservation: Warmth

One-on-one: Intimidation

The Enthusiast

Social: Sacrifice

Self-preservation: Network

One-on-one: Fascination

The Protector

Social: Solidarity

Self-preservation: Satisfaction

One-on-one: Possession

The Mediator

Social: Participation

Self-preservation: Appetite

One-on-one: Fusion

Center Points

Beyond the numbers and lines, the diagram is also divided into three triads or centers, which are heart, head, and body. These centers will further develop your personality by explaining your go-to emotions.

1. Heart Center

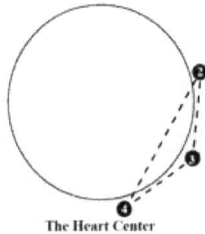

The Heart Center

The heart center focuses on numbers four, three, and two. Because the heart is often thought to be the leader of truth and emotions, these numbers represent someone who is usually more sensitive and strongly believes that we have to be honest about who we are. People who fall into the heart center feel a strong connection to the truth.

The go-to emotion for the heart center is shame. They are very concerned with their image and how other people view them. In fact, they are never truly happy with themselves unless they are able to see themselves through another person's eyes.

Like with the other two centers, the heart center has its strengths and weaknesses, however, these strengths and weaknesses will be determined based on which personality type you have. For example, type four's strengths will be different from type two's ("Heart Triad," n.d.).

Wing Points

The wing points are the parts of your personality which spread out to your two adjacent personality types (Cloete, n.d.). While these two types are not as big as your main personality type, they are important because they will balance out your personality. For instance, if you have a point four personality type, your adjacent type might be a point three.

These other types are sometimes known to contradict a person's personality but are important, so we can completely understand the whole of someone's personality. In fact, this is why there are tests and theories like the Enneagram. Not only does it allow us to get to know ourselves better, but it can help people, such as psychologists, who are trying to get to know us so they can help us too.

The question that a lot of people ask is whether we all have one wing or two wings. While this has brought on some controversy, many people believe that we do have two wings. Each point adjacent to our main personality type is one of our wings. Therefore, if you have a type nine personality, your wings will be type one and type eight. But, other people state this is not true and everyone has only one wing. There are other people who state that your wings are not specific to a certain personality type. They believe that because our personality has pieces from every number, then we have our main type and every other type is a wing to our personality, meaning we would have eight wings.

One important note to make about having different wings is that some wings are more dominant than others. If you haven't taken the Enneagram test yet, you will notice that when you get your results, they are laid out in a graph. This graph starts with your main personality as the strongest and then lists the other types of personalities from strongest to weakest. Most results will list all nine personality types.

Lines

One of the hardest parts of the Enneagram theory for people to understand is the lines within the theory. While I discussed the lines before, such as how they connect to the point, I will take this time to give you a bit more information on what the lines mean.

These lines are called the lines of influence or lines of movement (Cloete, n.d.). They are the way you will trace your personality through the Enneagram. Even though we have a main personality type, we can move around between the lines. Our main type will remain the same, however, the situations we go through in life and other factors will influence our journey on the lines throughout the Enneagram.

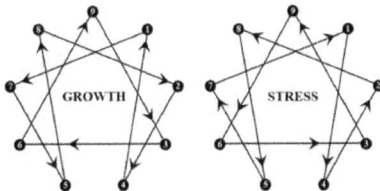

There are two types of lines. There is the line of stress and the line of growth. When you look at your main personality type on the Enneagram, you will see two lines with arrows. One arrow will be pointing away from your number type, which is called the line of growth. The other arrow will be pointing towards your number type and this is referred to as the line of stress.

When you think of the line of growth, you can think of releasing yourself from your unhealthy personality types. This is the line which moves us towards healthier parts of a personality. While we move along this line, we will release our stresses in life and move towards self-actualization (Cloete, n.d.).

The line of stress is the opposite of the line of growth. This line focuses on how we feel when we are under pressure or stressed. Often, these instances will make us pick up unhealthy lifestyle habits. At the same time, we can work to change the negatives into positives, which will often help balance us out as individuals (Cloete, n.d.).

Levels of Integration

Levels of integration are also known as levels of integration. Within each personality type, there are other pieces which make up the personality. These are similar to your behaviors, motivations, and attitude. Basically, these are the pieces which help make up your whole personality, similar to how pieces of the puzzle come together to create the whole puzzle.

When you start to understand these levels, you will come to realize that when people are changing, such as feeling more relaxed one moment and then anxious the next, they are going through different levels within their personality.

There are three levels of integration, which are healthy, average, and unhealthy (Cloete, n.d.). When people exhibit an unhealthy level of integration, they let their fears or other emotions control them. When people are at an average level of integration, the core problem is still a driving force in their behavior, however, they are able to let go of some core issues. When people are at a healthy level of integration, they can let go of the core emotions as they understand why these are occurring. This helps them move on, so they can find a healthier way to manage life stresses and situations. In a sense, they move beyond the limitations they believed they had.

Within these levels of integration are other levels and numbers associated with each level. Each level has three numbers, which correlate to how well the personality performs within its level of integration. These smaller levels are as follows:

In the healthy level, you can be a level one, two or three. Level one is at the level of a libertarian. Level two is at the level of psychological capacity and level three is at the level of social value ("How The System Works," n.d.).

In the average level, you can be a level four, five, or six. Level four is the level representing social role or imbalance. Level five is at the level of interpersonal control. Level six is at the level of overcompensation ("How The System Works," n.d.).

In the unhealthy level, you can be a level seven, eight, or nine. Level seven is a level of violation. Level eight is at the level of compulsion and obsession. Level nine is at the level of pathological destructiveness ("How The System Works," n.d.).

Benefits of the Enneagram

People often turn to the Enneagram to learn more about their personality for many reasons. While some people are curious about their personality type, other people want to know so they can better understand themselves or another person. Psychologists and other professionals often use the Enneagram to help them better understand their patients.

There are several benefits which can come from the Enneagram. Not only can this theory and test benefit people on an individual level, but also as a group.

Furthermore, the Enneagram can also benefit people on an organizational level.

Individual Level Benefits

•Help people understand why they are dealing with certain behavioral or emotional problems.

•Help people gain insight into their personality so they can understand themselves better.

•The Enneagram can help increase a person's confidence and motivation.

•The Enneagram can help increase a person's compassion for others.

•People can start to understand their previous behavioral patterns.

•The Enneagram can help people grow in general as they begin to understand their personality better.

Group Level Benefits

•The Enneagram can help decrease conflict within a group.

●It can also help each group member understand where another group member stands, why people act in certain ways, and where each member's strengths and weaknesses are.

●The Enneagram can help improve business processes.

●It can strengthen communication between team members, which will enhance other areas of the group.

Organizational Level Benefits

●The Enneagram can help limit the political atmosphere of an organization.

●It can improve the organization's leadership as a whole.

●The Enneagram can help the organization improve the emotions and fears associated with change.

The Enneagram is so much more than a diagram with lines, numbers, and arrows. It can also do more than to explain a person's personality. As you can see in the benefits above, the Enneagram can help people advance in many areas of their personal and professional life. Furthermore, the Enneagram can continue to help you as you develop through life's different stages.

Chapter 5: What Is The Enneagram?

The way our minds work out personality differences, the things that separate us from one another, the core of what makes us who we are can be a fascinating study. Yet, much of this can be explained by a unique analysis system called the Enneagram, the accuracy of which has been a marvel for millions of people. Amazed at how well it can determine a specific personality type and how easily it can predict behaviors has caused people to wonder if there was a spiritual element to the system.

The most fruitful applications of the Enneagram come from using it for growth. Observe the ways your personality's desires shape your actions. Notice when self-talk is monopolizing your attention, taking you out of the moment, and preventing you from fully engaging and use these moments of observation as a wake-up call to return your attention to the world around you and make active, conscious choices. It is up to you to take what you have learned from the Enneagram and apply it in the ways that best fit your personal needs and circumstances.

Most of us go through life trying to deal with its struggles, challenges, and demands utterly unaware of the fact that there is a difference between the true self and the personality ego self that deals with everyday living. To "be yourself" is easier to say than done in our society because we often are tangled up in mass consciousness and leave very little room for authentic self-expression and self-understanding. That is what the Enneagram is all about. It's a tool designed to help you simplify and increase your knowledge of self and in the process transcend your present level of human consciousness.

In a world layered with illusions, where everyone wears a mask on a daily basis, those who have grown tired of masquerades are thirsty for truth and authentic self-expression. This is not something new as the quest has been ongoing for centuries now. Since the time of Socrates and even further back, there have always been those seeking the real knowledge of who they are. However, something is changing in our society.

Unfortunately, few people are aware of this inner being and so fail to grasp its importance. In today's modern world, the majority of people are a product of their environment where the focus is on building up external connections while seeking personal fulfillment at the same time so they are not focused on feeding the inner person. In generations past, the concept of building up the spiritual person within was a normal part of human existence, but as times changed and more technology made life a world of immediate gratification, the idea of the spiritual person came to be viewed as something contrary to science.

It is not common to find environments today that actually support the idea of exploring one's spirituality and following its calling. Actually, it is more likely one will be mocked as being unenlightened and following archaic customs. Yet, for those who dare to explore it, this journey is one that actually makes it easier to fit into this modern world that we live in. Ironically, once we have come to understand our unique Enneagram personality, a natural extension of this knowledge allows us to have better relationships with others, to meet challenges more effectively, and to live on the surface with the rest of the world more comfortably. In essence, it makes those external connections easier and less daunting.

Every day people are in search of a deeper meaning in life. In our modern and progressive world, the automatic tendency is to look outside of ourselves for that sense of purpose, which is sad because the real answer to what makes us who we are has little to do with our external environment. So, while so many are searching to find their purpose in the praise of others, in thrill-seeking adventures life has to offer and even in the bottom of a bottle or drugs, many will be surprised to discover that the real answer to their true self is already within their possession.

While these external forms of stimulation and self-fulfillment can provide some level of support and personal edification, the positive results they provide are often fleeting. This is because they do not feed the inner core of our beings, the essence of who we are. Through the pages of this book, we begin to learn to see ourselves with the eyes of insight rather than through physical connections. It will give you crystal clarity as you begin to identify patterns within your own personal human nature that you never fully understood before.

If you want to be very honest with yourself, then learning how to identify and read Enneagram personalities is probably the single most important element that can connect you to the real inner being that lies hidden beneath the surface.

You will finally discover the real you and become empowered enough to discern the difference between the mask you have been wearing as a form of protection all your life and the real authentic self that is you. Not only will you learn more about yourself, but you will also begin to see the world with fresh new eyes, understanding why people think, feel, behave and act as they do. This will enable you to spot those that you are most compatible with and nurture more of those relationships.

Humanity is making a momentous leap in consciousness whereby as our lives become more complex, we experience the need to develop higher, better, more complex thinking and behaviors in order to cope. What most of us are discovering though is this approach is not working too well.

Have you reached a point in your life where the need to discover who you really are? Sometimes it can be tough understanding your own behavior and actions or why you react the way you do in certain situations. It is a very sobering moment when you wake up one day to the realization that you do not even know who you really are - deep inside. The pathway to the inner world is filled with great mystery and can often intimidate us especially when we have been locked out of our own truth for decades. That is where tools and proven systems become useful.

The Enneagram is an ancient system and tool that was created to help those of us who care about uncovering the layers of mass consciousness so we can dive deep to discover our true self. In addition, this book is designed to help make that journey of self-discovery and this ancient tool more straightforward, understandable, and quick to utilize.

Enneagram Personalities

If you are reading this book, chances are you have already heard something about the Enneagram personality but may not be entirely sure of what it is. While some people will say it is a complex system that is hard to understand, others believe it to be quite enlightening. It is true there is quite a mystery surrounding this iconic symbol, which leads many to ask deep and thought-provoking questions. Is it like the horoscope with deep mystical and symbolic meanings? Alternatively, is it a modern means of profiling people's psychological behaviors? Is it science or is it Spiritism? Does it really have practical applications or is it simply another fad of mythical proportions? All of those are legitimate questions that many new to the system are inclined to ask. So, what exactly is it and what is its real purpose? Why do we need it?

In short, the Enneagram is a means of giving you a chance to peek inside yourself to see who you really are at the core, to discover the kind of person you were meant to be and to help you to understand the other people who are sharing your personal environment together.

Even though we all live in the same world, we each see it from a different perspective. The main function of the Enneagram is not only to show you exactly how you view the world but also to give you some insight into how other people see it as well. It offers you valuable insight that can help you to become a better communicator and by extension help you to improve your work and social interactions when you are connected with those in your external environment.

As you learn the different personality types, you might find that it has a very effective means of allowing you to see deep below the surface so you can better understand exactly why people practice certain behaviors over and over again. However, it also goes a step further than that. It gives you the ability to break the mold that you may have been stuck in for years and put you on a separate growth path to a better way of life.

Still, with all the hype surrounding this new system of analyzing people, some may conclude that it is nothing more than a simple personality test. However, they would be wrong. While the Enneagram dates back for at least half a millennium, it has found a new and more practical use in today's modern world.

Its insights help you to make very practical life decisions; those that could land you a better job, an improved and enhanced lifestyle, one that best fits the kind of person you really are so you will be more fulfilled with the activities you choose to do. The more the Enneagram reveals your inner self to you, the calmer your life can become and the easier it will be to tap into your hidden talents and use them to enhance your life.

It is important, however, to understand that the true purpose of the Enneagram has nothing to do with self-improvement, which most people are seeking when they discover it. Rather, its primary goal is to transform your consciousness so that you can identify your true self. The benefit of building your character and improving relationships are merely a very positive side effect of that discovery of the inner person.

The real goal is to unite that inner person with a being that is higher than they are. To find a way of connecting yourself with a more spiritual existence is a key component in finding our own personal purpose and ourselves in life. This deeper connection knows no boundaries and is transmitted through a universal language that is not rooted in gender, religion, nationality, or culture.

You will find that each personality type is rooted in one of three centers of intelligence - the head, the heart, and the body. These centers dictate how we will relate to the external world. Even within these distinct types, you will find instinctual subtypes that can have a powerful influence on exactly how we interact with the world around us.

The key to making this happen, however, lies in our ability to understand what the symbol means and allowing it to move us to take specific actions that will put us on a better and more trustworthy path that will guide us in the direction we were meant to go.

Chapter 6: The Enneagram Of Personality

What Is The Enneagram?

As mentioned before, the Enneagram method of psyche development stems from a principle of integrated, or interconnected, personality types. This investigation of the psyche stems from the premise of nine separate personality types, referred to as "Enneatypes," which are assigned to the nine points of the Enneagram symbol. These points are drawn interconnectedly and define the connections and combinations of how these Enneatypes can be understood and can be worked together to further the development of the psyche of any individual willing to put in the work and effort needed for personal growth and development.

Understanding is the key element in working with the Enneagram. It can aid on many different levels, including personal, interpersonal, professional, and spiritual, among others. It offers paths to enlightenment, self-awareness, and self-development. These Enneatypes are said manifest in human nature as nine divine qualities that represent the whole of personal existence.

The Russian mystic Gurdjieff describes the Enneagram philosophy as perpetual motion that unfolds creation and uses a series of movement and dance to connect even deeper to that underlying principle of development.

While the Enneagram is a philosophy of personality typing that is used in multiple areas, including an examination of the applications as could be applied to the personality types in the psychological realms of the DSM-1 (The Diagnostic and Statistical Manual of Mental Disorders), as purported by Dr. Marlene Cresci Cohen, the true depth to be found within the Enneagram can be found in its substantial development nature as applies to spiritual growth and achievement. Almost all forms of Enneagram programs to be found have extremely strong inclinations toward the spiritual ramifications of higher awareness.

As such, the Enneagram is not only a tool used for personal transformation, but ideally, it is one that can contribute to an even higher level to collective transformation. It is a dynamic system that can help you to understand the personality patterns for yourself, and help to identify them in others, to better assist you in finding ways to connect at a higher level.

The Enneagram theory is not just a simplistic one of learning more about yourself, but rather it is a theory to peel aside the many-faceted layers that make up the psyche of yourself and the others around you. You will learn not only how to work within your personality type and those of others but also how to travel around the circle to give more completeness of being to your existence and in your integration and associations with others.

The Enneagram Theory for Development

The Enneagram theory, as it applies to the development of ourselves first, is one of examining where we are at the moment in the nine-point system. It also takes a look at which points we go to when in times of stress, or those types of bad habits or influences we allow to affect us when we are in an unhealthy state. Transversely, the system also takes a look at where we go to in times of security or the types of good habits or influences that we allow to affect us when we are in a healthier state of being.

It is a strong tool for self-awareness and self-knowledge. But as with anything that causes us to turn inward, the work needing to be done to heal ourselves and bring us to a higher state of being can be very demanding, and sometimes even painful. This is not a theory that labels you and then permanently sticks you with that label. The Enneagram helps to open new pathways and processes to higher learning and awareness. It is not about sticking you in a single zone, but rather, it teaches you to get "unstuck" from wherever or whichever point you may currently find yourself within.

The Enneagram is empowering, teaching you how to understand how and why you react to certain situations and people in the way that you do, and then to take responsibility for your actions and behaviors and transform them into something far more powerful to help you move through life, and to stop hurting not only others, but to stop hurting yourself in the process.

We are all individuals. We act and react in certain ways. We are all valid individuals with validity to the way we feel. However, we all have experienced life and negative things, and even positive things have impacted and perhaps even tainted the way we respond to the world around us. It is time to take a serious look at ourselves if we truly want to expand into the ultimate collective consciousness.

The Enneagram is about finding your true self and learning how to forgive that self to grow. Each step on the journey is one of discovery and insight into who you are and who those around you are as well. The Enneagram teaches us not only that we react to events, but that in reality, we are reacting to our *perception* of those. How we perceive what happens around us is based on our puzzling through those things that have happened in the past, and assigning an assumption based on where we are in that perception. We come to learn that perception is not always reality. All too often, reality and our perception of it are not even close. By learning the how and why we do perceive things, and react like this to them, we can come closer to reality, which brings us closer to the collective consciousness and ultimately, closer to the Divine.

Understanding ourselves through the Enneagram is not only about discovering the good side inherent in our nature based on where we are at on our individual journeys, but also discovering the bad sides, the darkness within us. It is only by discovering these aspects of self that we can ultimately transform and heal ourselves, our lives, and the world around us.

The basis of the Enneagram starts with the premise that we develop our personality type based on events that have shaped who we have become from the inherent factors attributed to us even before our time of birth, through childhood and adolescence, up to our present-day selves. But this is only the beginning, defining the concept of our "Basic Self." What we do with that self is up to us. Our Basic Self also fluctuates through different aspects based on healthy and unhealthy life points and experiences and can climb up and down the developmental ladder within each Enneatype. This simple ladder can take us through the stages of development in our lives from unhealthy aspects, through average aspects of self, all the way up through the higher, healthier levels that are the ideal to achieve.

There are no "good" or "bad" personality types. They all have ideals within them that may be more appealing at one point in your life or another, or that society may prefer, based on where we are at in our societal development. Every Enneatype has a purpose and a range of unhealthy to healthy behavioral traits and the way we respond to situations. Not all Enneatypes may respond to situations in the same way.

Take the time to discover who you are, based on the Enneagram, and utilize the teachings within to enrich yourself, your life, your relationships to others, and your relationship to the world around you.

There is no right or wrong way. There are no judgments. There is only doing the work as you see needed, independent of what others think or believe. The Enneagram is about you… and ultimately your connection to the Divine and to the divine nature within.

Chapter 7: Applying Your Gifts Every Day

As you continue practicing how to develop your empathic gifts, you are going to want to start learning about how you can apply them in your everyday life. This chapter is going to show you how you can begin taking your development to the next level and experiencing significantly more joy and empowerment from your empathic gifts. This level of integration is going to help you begin to overcome some of those more challenging symptoms you have been experiencing in your life so that you can start enjoying yourself once more.

Finding Where Your Day Can Be Improved

The first thing you are going to need to do in order to integrate your empathic gifts into your daily life is to start looking out for areas where your day can be improved. As an empath, you may be so used to living your days stressed out and overwhelmed that you may not even be clear as to where or when those feelings start to leak into your daily experiences. Getting clear on where these energies are coming from, when, why, and how it feels when they begin is going to help you get clear on what it is that you want to improve with your daily integration.

Keeping an empathic journal is a great way for you to start identifying areas of your life where you are being impacted by your gifts so that you know where you want to place your focus when it comes to intentionally incorporating them. You can keep just a small journal with you or even a note in your phone, where you will record the time of day when the energy came up, what was happening, what you were thinking, and how you were feeling. After a while, you will start to see trends in your energy, where your energy is absorbing unwanted energies, and how you might be leaving yourself vulnerable to these particular forms of energy.

Giving Yourself Permission to Start One Step at a Time

The next step in incorporating your empathic gifts into your daily life is giving yourself permission to do it at your own pace. One of the biggest mistakes empaths make is trying to change their entire lives in one go which, while admirable, can be extremely exhausting and overwhelming. The truth is, as you go about using your gift to empower you rather than allowing others to use it to exploit you, there is going to be some difficulties for you to endure. You are going to have to start learning how to navigate the energies of people as they grow frustrated with their newfound inability to exploit you, which takes some time to get used to. At first, you might find yourself giving in despite having all of the best practices in place and this can bring about frustration and anger within you, as well as the need to ground from the unwanted energies of the other person. Giving yourself permission to go slowly and make mistakes along the way ensures that you do not set your expectations too high and bite off more than you can reasonably chew.

The best way to give yourself permission and really mean it is to first declare that you are giving yourself permission to take things slowly and at your own pace. Then, create a mantra that you will use any time that you are actively put in a position where you need to give yourself permission to slow down and navigate it at your own pace. For example, if you are in a situation where you habitually find yourself letting others take advantage of you, give yourself permission to navigate it at your own pace and do your best to change the situation as much as possible.

If you find yourself struggling to make changes, take the pressure off by letting yourself know that there is no need to get it perfect the first time. The more you practice putting up shields and setting boundaries, the easier it will be for you to do so with greater assertiveness and intention in the future. There is nothing wrong with going slow and at your own pace, and do not be afraid to repeat your personal mantra to yourself anytime you start feeling like this is not true. Be gentle with yourself.

Steps to Integrating Your Empathic Gifts Daily

You are now ready to see what it looks like to start integrating your empathic gifts into your daily life! What this will look like from day to day will vary, depending on what situations you are entering and what is expected of you during these situations. For that reason, rather than giving you a routine or schedule for how you can incorporate your empathic gifts into every single day, I am going to give you some tips you can use to start incorporating it in unique experiences. Then, you can start relying on these anytime you need them to help you navigate new situations and experience greater comfort and empowerment in your life!

Step 1: Read the Energy of the Day

The first thing you can do each morning, aside from creating your shield and grounding yourself, is read the energy of that day. Many empaths report being able to feel the energy of any given day based on the energy that the general collective is giving off. Spending some time reading that energy each morning can help you get a sense of what you might stand to face as you go about your daily experiences.

You can read the energy of any given day during your morning meditation by simply asking your intuition what energies are present that day and how they may impact you. Then, trust any information that comes through intuitively, even if it does not necessarily make sense to you at that time. You may not have any words you can use to verbally describe what the energy is like, but instead, you may have a general feeling inside that gives you an idea of what to expect. This is plenty enough to give you an idea of what energies to look out for and how you may be able to prepare yourself against them, simply by being able to expect that they will arise.

Step 2: Read the Energy of People

The next thing that you can consider doing on a daily basis is reading the energy of the people you encounter. Slowing down at the beginning of every interaction and taking a few moments to read the energy of the people around you will give you an opportunity to get an idea of how they may be feeling that day. This is going to help you not only get a sense for how your interactions may be, but also for where energy may be coming if you start to experience unexpected energies in your own body. For example, if you know that your spouse was particularly happy that morning and you have an unexplained feeling of elation all day long, it may be the energy that you picked up on from your spouse.

You can also use this as an opportunity to read the energy of new people that you encounter to help you determine whether or not they are a good person to engage and interact with. If you are looking to make new friends or network with new people, for example, you can use your intuition to help you determine whether or not it will be a positive experience. This is a great way to start picking up on the energy of energy parasites such as narcissists early on so that you can avoid building relationships with them right from the start.

Step 3: Create a Safe Grounding Space for Yourself

You likely already crave solitude to some degree, so why not feed into that desire and create a safe grounding space for yourself? You can do this by either creating a grounding sanctuary within your home or by finding a place outside of your home that you like to retreat to. Or, if you want to get really fancy, you can do both!

If you want to create a grounding sanctuary in your home, consider choosing one room or an area in one room where you can fill it with things that are relaxing and grounding. Use crystals, live plants, calming incenses, soft fabrics, uplifting pictures, and other great and relaxing tools to help you make the area more inviting. Then, begin practicing your daily grounding experiences in that specific area in your home every single time. What will end up happening is that you find yourself connecting more deeply with that particular area, so just entering it will be grounding, thus making intentional grounding meditations in that sanctuary even more powerful.

If you would like to incorporate a destination into your grounding experiences, consider choosing one that is nearby and that you can attend frequently. A local park or a bird sanctuary may be a great opportunity for you to find a local place that you can retreat to and experience grounding energies in. This type of grounding destination can be particularly helpful if you are someone who finds that their own home tends to become overwhelmed with exhausting or troublesome energies.

Step 4: Make Experiences Richer

One great way that you can incorporate your gift into your daily life is through making your experiences richer using your extra senses. Think of it this way: if you can experience someone else's energies and emotions that deeply, imagine what else you can experience that deeply? See how intensely you can experience meals, laughter, nostalgia, and tranquility. Look for opportunities to uplift yourself through these experiences and see if you can find ones that routinely makes you feel better, particularly if you are having a difficult day. In doing so, not only does this become a fun opportunity for you to experience life more joyously, but it also allows you to begin finding experiences that can reliably lift you out of a troublesome mood.

Your Quick Start Action Step: Experience Intensely

Your quick action step today is to find one experience that you can fully immerse yourself into and let yourself be swept away from it just like you are by other people's energies or emotions when you are not grounded and protected. Find one activity that you can fully immerse yourself into, and see just how much energy you can draw out of that experience and what that energy feels like. If it begins to feel too intense or overwhelming, take a few minutes to ground yourself before either going back into the activity or switching to something more calming.

The more you practice getting the most out of life by experiencing energies in this positive way, the better your life is going to feel overall. It is well worth your time to start learning how to become deeply mindful of and engaged in each moment in your life so that you can stop retreating and dissociating from your experiences. This is going to help you reconnect with your daily life and start living for you again, and not for everyone around you.

Chapter 8: What Is Sacred Enneagram

The Enneagram is a personality typing system that consists of the following main components:

- 9 personality types
- 3 centers of intelligence
- 18 wings
- 27 sub-types
- 3 triadic styles

An Enneagram itself is a nine-pointed geometric figure. It looks like a circle marked with nine equidistant points. Each point on the Enneagram has a number from 1-9 assigned to it. The number 9 can be found at the top of the Enneagram, and from there, numbers continue in a clockwise pattern beginning with the number 1. Solid inner lines connect all nine numbers on the Enneagram. Below you will find an example of a basic Enneagram symbol.

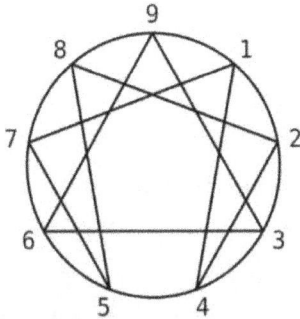

You will see from this diagram that on an Enneagram, the numbers 3, 6, and 9 form an equilateral triangle. There are further connections within this symbol such as the following: 1 connects with 4, 4 connects with 2, 2 connects with 8, 8 connects with 5, 5 connects with 7 and 7 connects with 1. This pattern is standard on all Enneagrams.

The word Enneagram comes from the Greek word "ennea" meaning "nine" and "gramma" meaning "figure." In this case, "figure" means something that is written down or drawn. In the context of psychology, the Enneagram has become a framework used to map out nine possible personality types.

The "Enneagram of personality" suggests that there are nine distinct strategies or styles of relating to self, to others, and to the world as a whole. It is proposed that each personality type has its own way of thinking and feeling and that these patterns of behavior come from deep inner motivations and fears. The nine distinct personality types recognized by Enneagram are each represented by a specific point on the Enneagram symbol.

Each of the nine types is associated with a specific style, motivation, fear, and level of health.

Use of the Enneagram can aid in your quest to learn more about yourself and your patterns of behavior. The first step in your journey of self-discovery will be to determine your personality type based on the Enneagram. Understanding your type in relationships with others can offer insight and a "map" to your own personal development. When you dive into this type of self-exploration, it can help you uncover the impact that your motivations, attitudes, and fears may be having on your thoughts and your decisions. You will begin to understand how your motivations and desires have been influencing your actions and reactions. With this increased knowledge comes the opportunity for growth and true integration of self.

The Enneagram assessment has some similarities to other personality tests, such as the DISC assessments, Strength finders, and the Myer-Briggs. What makes the Enneagram different is that it focuses more on motivation than on behavior. It is not a strict or rule-bound system. Assigning you to a specific personality "type" is not meant to bind or restrict you. Enneagram teachings suggest that the point is not to put people in boxes, but to do quite the opposite. The idea is to free people from the limitations and habits that they continue to put themselves into.

The teachings of the Enneagram can help you uncover the roots of many of your motivations, desires, fears, and coping strategies. It can help you figure out what you wish for and want, what you value the most in life, and what you are most tempted by. It can help you learn what your greatest strengths and virtues are, and also highlights the things that you might be most afraid of. On this journey, you will also uncover what your biggest faults and weaknesses might be, and which behaviors may be holding you back.

Enneagram discovery is about recognizing what drives you at your core and getting to know yourself from the inside. The key concept is that by understanding these things about yourself, you can change what you need to and further your own personal development.

The Enneagram challenges you to explore who you really are. It gives you a glimpse into both your true self and your false self. By learning about your Enneagram type, you will discover some of your potential blind spots and weaknesses. You will learn about your default coping strategies, and why these might not be working for you. Enneagram exploration can help you figure out why you keep making the same mistakes, and how best to overcome your self-defeating patterns of behavior. Learning about your blind spots can increase the level of compassion that you have towards yourself and can help you love yourself for who you really are.

A unique contribution of the Enneagram is that it not only teaches you who you are right now but also points out who you have the potential to be. Enneagram teaches you how you perceive your reality, and how you can learn to adjust your point of view. The teachings of the Enneagram help break down your personality and habits bit by bit so that you can get past your own limitations. By giving you the chance to explore ways of better understanding and improving yourself, it offers you the opportunity to become who you were meant to be.

It is widely recognized in Enneagram teachings that people generally do not change their "type." They can, however, grow, adapt, and develop into the person they were destined to be.

An added benefit of the Enneagram typing system is that it allows people to feel like they are part of a group. Some people grow quite proud of, and open to sharing, their Enneagram number. It is generally easy for people to understand and relate to labels such as these. Human beings generally prefer absolutes to uncertainty, and many people seem to appreciate the numbers associated with Enneagram. It reminds them that there are others in the world who are similar to them and that other people think and feel the same way that they do. This tool reminds them that as humans, we are all flawed.

An Enneagram is a dynamic tool, but like all personality systems, it has its limitations. The truth remains that not all parts of human personality and relationships can be completely understood.

Below is a summary of some of the greatest benefits of understanding your Enneagram type:

• Helps you improve your interpersonal relationships

• Leads to a better understanding of the people in your life

- Helps give direction to your life and increase your motivation to change

- Identifies negative behavior patterns that you have been relying on

- Helps you figure out a better, healthier way of responding to stress

- Increases your self-awareness and self-confidence

- Identifies your needs and weaknesses and teaches you ways of improving

- Identifies your strengths and unique abilities and how to use them

- Teaches you to live your life to the fullest, and to be as happy as you can be

- Decreases self-doubt, self-criticism, and other negative thought patterns

- Helps you grow into the best version of yourself that you can be

- Helps you understand and deal with your core motivational issues

- Helps you understand your dysfunctional behaviors

• Increases your compassion and empathy towards others

• Uncovers your pathways to further self-development

• Increases leadership abilities and authenticities

• Reduces judgment and criticism of others

• Builds your understanding and tolerance of others

• Improves your communication skills and abilities

• Helps determine your creative or professional options

Chapter 9: What Is The Enneagram?

The way our minds work out personality differences, the things that separate us from one another, the core of what makes us who we are can be a fascinating study. Yet, much of this can be explained by a unique analysis system called the Enneagram, the accuracy of which has been a marvel for millions of people. Amazed at how well it can determine a specific personality type and how easily it can predict behaviors has caused people to wonder if there was a spiritual element to the system.

The most fruitful applications of the Enneagram come from using it for growth. Observe the ways your personality's desires shape your actions. Notice when self-talk is monopolizing your attention, taking you out of the moment, and preventing you from fully engaging and use these moments of observation as a wake-up call to return your attention to the world around you and make active, conscious choices. It's up to you to take what you've learned from the Enneagram and apply it in the ways that best fit your personal needs and circumstances.

Most of us go through life trying to deal with its struggles, challenges, and demands utterly unaware of the fact that there is a difference between the true self and the personality ego self that deals with everyday living. To "be yourself" is easier to say than done in our society because we often get tangled up in mass consciousness and leave very little room for authentic self-expression and self-understanding. That's what the Enneagram is all about. It's a tool designed to help you simplify and increase your knowledge of self and in the process transcend your present level of human consciousness.

In a world layered with illusions, where everyone wears a mask on a daily basis, those who've grown tired of masquerades are thirsty for truth and authentic self-expression. This isn't something new as the quest has been ongoing for centuries now. Since the time of Socrates and even further back, there have always been those seeking the real knowledge of who they are. However, something is changing in our society.

Unfortunately, few people are aware of this inner being and so fail to grasp its importance. In today's modern world, the majority of people are a product of their environment where the focus is on building up external connections while seeking personal fulfillment at the same time so they are not focused on feeding the inner person. In generations past, the concept of building up the spiritual person within was a normal part of human existence, but as times changed and more technology made life a world of immediate gratification, the idea of the spiritual person came to be viewed as something contrary to science.

It is not common to find environments today that actually support the idea of exploring one's spirituality and following its calling. As a matter of fact, it is more likely one will be mocked as being unenlightened and following archaic customs. Yet, for those who dare to explore it, this journey is one that actually makes it easier to fit into this modern world that we live in. Ironically, once we have come to understand our unique Enneagram personality, a natural extension of this knowledge allows us to have better relationships with others, to meet challenges more effectively, and to live on the surface with the rest of the world more comfortably. In essence, it makes those external connections easier and less daunting.

Every day people are in search of a deeper meaning in life. In our modern and progressive world, the automatic tendency is to look outside of ourselves for that sense of purpose which is sad because the real answer to what makes us who we are has little to do with our external environment. So, while so many are searching to find their purpose in the praise of others, in thrill-seeking adventures life has to offer and even in the bottom of a bottle or drugs, many will be surprised to discover that the real answer to their true self is already within their possession.

While these external forms of stimulation and self-fulfillment can provide some level of support and personal edification, the positive results they provide are often fleeting. This is because they don't feed the inner core of our beings, the essence of who we are. Through the pages of this book, we begin to learn to see ourselves with the eyes of insight rather than through physical connections. It will give you crystal clarity as you begin to identify patterns within your own personal human nature that you never fully understood before.

If you want to be totally honest with yourself, then learning how to identify and read Enneagram personalities is probably the single most important element that can connect you to the real inner being that lies hidden beneath the surface.

You will finally discover the real you and become empowered enough to discern the difference between the mask you've been wearing as a form of protection all your life and the real authentic self that is you. Not only will you learn more about yourself, but you'll also begin to see the world with fresh new eyes, understanding why people think, feel, behave and act as they do. This will enable you to spot those that you are most compatible with and nurture more of those relationships.

Humanity is making a momentous leap in consciousness whereby as our lives become more complex, we experience the need to develop higher, better, more complex thinking and behaviors in order to cope. What most of us are discovering though is this approach isn't working too well.

The best way to thrive as the world continues to make a global shift isn't to seek more complicated coping mechanisms to tackle the new emerging world, but rather to simplify the way we relate to and partner up with life. In other words, we realize the better option is to seek simple solutions to our complex problems. We are learning to prioritize and appreciate this quest for truth and have become curious to discover if indeed there is more to us than what we've grown to believe about ourselves.

Have you reached a point in your life where the need to discover who you really are? Sometimes it can be tough understanding your own behavior and actions or why you react the way you do in certain situations. It's a very sobering moment when you wake up one day to the realization that you don't even know who you really are - deep inside. The pathway to the inner world is filled with great mystery and can often intimidate us especially when we've been locked out of our own truth for decades. That's where tools and proven systems become useful.

The Enneagram is an ancient system and tool that was created to help those of us who care about uncovering the layers of mass consciousness so we can dive deep to discover our true self. And this book is designed to help make that journey of self-discovery and this ancient tool more straightforward, understandable, and quick to utilize.

Enneagram Personalities

If you're reading this book, chances are you've already heard something about the Enneagram personality but may not be entirely sure of what it is. While some people will say it is a complex system that is hard to understand, others believe it to be quite enlightening. It is true there is quite a mystery surrounding this iconic symbol which leads many to ask deep and thought-provoking questions. Is it like the horoscope with deep mystical and symbolic meanings? Or is it a modern means of profiling people's psychological behaviors? Is it science or is it spiritism? Does it really have practical applications or is it simply another fad of mythical proportions? All of those are legitimate questions that many new to the system are inclined to ask. So, what exactly is it and what is its real purpose? Why do we need it?

In short, the Enneagram is a means of giving you a chance to peek inside yourself to see who you really are at the core, to discover the kind of person you were meant to be and to help you to understand the other people who are sharing your personal environment together.

Even though we all live in the same world, we each see it from a different perspective. The main function of the Enneagram is not only to show you exactly how you view the world but also to give you some insight into how other people see it as well. It offers you valuable insight that can help you to become a better communicator and by extension help you to improve your work and social interactions when you are connected with those in your external environment.

As you learn the different personality types, you might find that it has a very effective means of allowing you to see deep below the surface so you can better understand exactly why people practice certain behaviors over and over again. But it also goes a step further than that. It gives you the ability to break the mold that you may have been stuck in for years and put you on a separate growth path to a better way of life.

Still, with all the hype surrounding this new system of analyzing people, some may conclude that it is nothing more than a simple personality test. But they would be wrong. While the Enneagram dates back for at least half a millennium, it has found a new and more practical use in today's modern world.

Its insights help you to make very practical life decisions; those that could land you a better job, an improved and enhanced lifestyle, one that best fits the kind of person you really are so you will be more fulfilled with the activities you choose to do. The more the Enneagram reveals your inner self to you, the calmer your life can become and the easier it will be to tap into your hidden talents and use them to enhance your life.

It is important, however, to understand that the true purpose of the Enneagram has nothing to do with self-improvement which most people are seeking when they discover it. Rather, its primary goal is to transform your consciousness so that you can identify your true self. The benefit of building your character and improving relationships are merely a very positive side effect of that discovery of the inner person.

The real goal is to unite that inner person with a being that is higher than themselves. To find a way of connecting yourself with a more spiritual existence is a key component in finding ourselves and our own personal purpose in life. This deeper connection knows no boundaries and is transmitted through a universal language that is not rooted in gender, religion, nationality, or culture.

You'll find that each personality type is rooted in one of three centers of intelligence - the head, the heart, and the body. These centers dictate how we will relate to the external world. Even within these distinct types, you'll find instinctual subtypes that can have a powerful influence on exactly how we interact with the world around us.

The key to making this happen, however, lies in our ability to understand what the symbol means and allowing it to move us to take specific actions that will put us on a better and more trustworthy path that will guide us in the direction we were meant to go.

Chapter 10: Type Three: The Performer

Overview

When the Performer is at their best, they are primed to accomplish some of the greatest achievements possible for mankind. They are the jewels of humanity and, as such, they are often the source of great admiration on the part of others— not only because of their personal achievements, but because of their kind and gracious manner. Balanced Performers know how good it can feel to keep on improving themselves in order to stretch towards greater accomplishments. They thrive when they are able to contribute their impressive abilities to the society around them. Better yet, they also appreciate being able to motivate other people to be the best possible version of themselves that they can be. The Performer is a person who tends to be well liked and even popular among their friends. They would be the student that is often elected "class president" or "home coming queen" because their positive energy makes people want to associate with them—even to the point of using them as a personal avatar. A healthy performer is able to embody everything that is the best in a given culture. This means that others are able to see their aspirations and dreams mirrored in their image.

Like a confident actor, Performers truly believe in themselves and think that they deserve to develop themselves into even better versions of the people that they are. This makes them the most successful and well liked of all the types, in general. Healthy Performers can serve as a living, breathing role model because they are able to embody socially valued qualities to an impressive degree. Because healthy Performers sincerely believe they are worth the effort that it would take to become the best that they can be. They are often successful in obtaining their goals. When things are going well and working according to nature, their impressive success can work to inspire the people around them to invest more in their own self- care and self- development.

A Performer is relentless in their pursuit of success. That sense of success is determined not by some intrinsic belief, as in the case of the Perfectionist discussed above. Their notion of success comes from outside sources, whether it is defined by their family, their culture, and their social setting. This could mean trying to acquire the most luxurious material possessions and economic status symbols, such as the biggest house, the fattest wallet or the flashiest car. It could also mean achieving other kinds of success, for example, in the realm of knowledge. If they come from an academic family, they might try to distinguish themselves in a university setting or in a medical laboratory. Often, as the name suggests, the Performer desires to become famous, whether as an actor, a fashion model, an artist, writer or public figure. Performers frequently are politicians, comedians or other kinds of public speakers. In a religious family, this could manifest itself in terms of encouragement to become a community leader, whether it be a minister, a priest, or a rabbi, professions that all carry a certain status. Regardless of how each Performer understands success, they will always try to achieve recognition. The worst thing that could happen to a Performer is that they feel like they are a nobody.

Because of these compulsions, Performers learn as children to act in ways that earn them positive attention and words of praise from the adults around them—they will become particularly attached to any adult who lavishes the most excessive words upon them, whether or not they are sincere. Whatever activities appear to be recognized as most valuable by their social circle are the things that Performers most want to do, and they put a seemingly unending amount of energy into excelling at those things. Performers also learn as children how to support and develop whatever about them receives notice from respected members of their community.

While it is certainly true that all human beings need love, attention, support, and the affirmation of their self-worth in order to truly thrive, the Performer is undoubtedly the type that most exemplifies this universal social drive. The Performer does not want success because of what it can allow them to buy (like sevens), nor for the power and feeling of independence that they hope it will bring (like eights). Instead, they truly desire success because they are afraid that without it, they will be destined to vanish into an abyss of nothingness and worthlessness. Performers feel that they are no one, unless they receive the burst of positive attention brought by success and accomplishment.

This is also where the Performers run into their worst source of trouble. Because they will do anything in order to accomplish the thing that promises to make them feel a higher sense of self-worth, the Performer faces a sincere risk of becoming alienated—even to the point that they lose any sense of their true identity and purpose, their authentic feelings and their actual interests. When they are in this unbalanced state, it is easy to deceive a Performer, allowing them to easily fall prey to scams and con artists. Beyond all of this risk, the Performer actually faces a deeper problem, which is the fact that their search for a way to be of worth helps form a vicious downwards spiral, as it continues to take them further and further away from their own true self where their core of real value resides. This process usually starts during their childhood years when the Performer starts to become dependent on receiving attention from those around them and in embracing the qualities rewarded by others. This causes them to gradually lose touch with themselves, which usually manifests itself during their teenage rebellious years. The more they embrace the qualities valued by others, the more they leave behind their true, inner self, until one day they wake up and realize they do not even know who that self is or how to help it.

Because of this gradual sense of loss, the Performer is a paradoxical type. Although they are the primary type in the Heart Center, the Performer is not considered by others to be a "feeling" person. Instead, they are always perceived to be people of relentless action and achievement. This is likely because they put their feelings away in a box in order to allow themselves to try to get ahead with what they are aiming to achieve in life. The Performer is so committed to their performance that they are willing to suppress their emotions that they view as an impediment. In the place of feelings, they embrace thinking and practical actions.

The Performer often has trouble when someone makes them acknowledge how much they have shaped their lives to the expectations of other people. They often have trouble taking the next step forward to understand what they actually want because they often simply have no idea. Even though it is a very common question, it was not one that they remembered ever tackling before. With all of this in mind, we can say that the underlying problem that the unhealthy Performer faces is that they have not been given permission to try to be who they really are and, therefore, they have repressed their own authentic qualities. As young children, they were repeatedly given the message that they could not possess disruptive feelings and just be themselves. Acceptance only came when they were able to put on the socially prescribed mask. This, of course, is a basic problem faced by all members of society. However, because of the particular background and makeup of the Performer, they are extremely susceptible to these messages. They live and breathe them until they accept them as their unquestioned, unquestionable truth. Fortunately, however, this need to people please means that Performers may be easier to convince to accept help than other types; whether they are able to actually do the necessary work to truly achieve happiness is an open question.

The connected types of the Performer are:

Wing: Giver 2

Wing: Romantic 4

Security Type: Loyal Skeptic 6

Stress Type: Mediator 9

The most common non-connected types of the Performer are:

Epicure 7

Perfectionist 1

Protector 8

The probability of types (other types to consider if Performer is your top choice):

54% Performer 3

13% Epicure 7

9% Perfectionist 1

7% Giver 2

5% Protector 8

5% Mediator 9

If you scored high on the Performer test, you have a 54% probability that this is your type. However, you should consult your second and third top scores to see if you might be an Epicure, Perfectionist, Giver, Protector or Mediator as these types can often be confused. Remember, if a certain type has a strong wing of one or the other, that can greatly influence how the personality manifests itself. If you cannot accept the type you are, your feelings may be legitimate, or could be a result of the negative stereotypes you have heard about the type, so make sure to explore any strong reactions you may have.

Myths About the Performer

The most negative stereotypes about the Performer is that they are self-absorbed, egotistical and uninterested in other people, yet they can be very caring and are full of initiative—including helping others. The Performer can be seen as deceptive, but they do not deceive in order to hurt other people because they are unsure of their true identity and thus often shift their behaviors as they search for it.

Adjectives used for the Performer

Optimistic, energetic, confident, enthusiastic, industrious, practical, grounded and fast-paced are the positive adjectives. Impatient, rushed, self-aggrandizing, vindictive, vain, superficial, workaholic pretentious and competitive are the negative adjectives.

The Underlying Truths of the Performer

The basic principle the Performer has forgotten: Natural laws will enable all things to work as they should.

The Performer wrongly believes: It is necessary to avoid failure at all costs. All people must work alone and for themselves. Rewards come thanks to actions not identity.

The Performer created these behaviors to compensate: Working for approval in order to feel loved and, thus, covering their true desires and needs.

The Characteristics that Define the Performer

Because of these adaptive behaviors, the perfectionist focuses on: Getting things done, being the best at all times, being the most efficient person possible.

They put their energy into: Accomplishing goals, staying busy, getting recognition for their accomplishments, self-promotion and looking as good as possible.

They desperately try to avoid: Failure, embarrassment, uncomfortable feelings, exhibiting doubt, slowing down and being incapable of doing things.

They have these strengths: Being an enthusiastic, capable, well liked leader. Being practical, inspirational and put together.

They communicate in the following way: With direct, easy to understand language that might veer into impatience or insensitivity.

The Sources of Stress, Anger and Defensiveness

They are stressed by: All the pressure to always get things done, achieve more, and obtain a higher status and value; the fear of failure.

They are angered about: Anything that gets in their way, including incompetent and inefficient people.

They are defensive towards: Criticism from others, especially those they do not respect highly.

Their anger and defensiveness are characterized as such: Occasional irritable outbursts, frequent signs of impatience.

Personal Growth

Their final goal is: To accept being loved regardless of their achievements.

They can further this growth by:

Being mindful when they postpone feelings ("I'll be happy when…").

Taking advantage of their natural resilience, optimism and flexibility.

Their biggest obstacle is:

Avoiding constant comparisons with others.

Feeling like they always have to perform.

Not reacting aggressively when they detect incompetent behavior in others.

Knowing when to stop.

Noticing when fantasies of success become more important than actual abilities.

Others can support this growth by:

Helping them recognize limits and leaving time for their emotions to surface before they run off to accomplish the next task on their list.

Keeping them grounded and not dominated by fantasy.

Providing support in making choices based on feelings rather than desire for status.

Reminding them they are loved for who they are not for what they do.

Discouraging comparisons between them and others.

Allowing them to have down time and not always feel like they have to perform.

Famous Performers

(including some of the most influential politicians, speakers and actors, but also some infamous, duplicitous criminals):

Oprah Winfrey, Bill Clinton, Deepak Chopra, O.J. Simpson, Michael Jordan, Paul McCartney, Elvis Presley, Will Smith, Courtney Cox, Jon Bon Jovi, Bernie Madoff, John Edwards, Taylor Swift, Tiger Woods, Ken Watanabe, Richard Gere, Justin Bieber, Truman Capote, Emperor Constantine, Madonna, Ben Kingsley, Demi Moore, Lance Armstrong, Jamie Foxx, Andy Warhol, Tony Robbins, Barbra Streisand, Augustus Caesar, Tony Blair, Prince William, Arnold Schwarzenegger, Carl Lewis, Muhammed Ali, Mitt Romney, Bill Wilson (AA Founder), Whitney Houston, Lady Gaga, Brooke Shields, Cindy Crawford, Tom Cruise, Kevin Spacey and Anne Hathaway.

Related Types

Every personality type is influenced by the wings to the point that they might blend into one of them. If a personality type has a strong wing, it will make a huge impact on the individual's personality.

Giver 2 (wing): When a Performer has a more developed 2 wing, they can be seductive, sociable and popular. These two types are even more closely related than other types because they belong to the same Heart Center type, which causes them to share certain personality traits. Because Givers and Performers both tend to be "doers," they are full of energy and eager to get things done. They share a high degree of energy and a willingness to adapt to anything they face. These two types differ since Performers are more intent on getting things done while Givers are always thinking about other people's needs and wants.

Romantic 4 (wing): When a Performer has a more developed 4 wing, they can be introspective, artistic and pretentious. The Romantic and the Performer are even more closely related than other related types because they share the same Heart Center types. They both are obsessed with getting other people's approval and recognition. Their intense creativity helps them in their work, but they both can be competitive. Their differences are that Performers are always focused on a future goal while Romantics are less so since they are often distracted by their inner focus.

Loyal Skeptic 6 (security type): These types are closely related because the Performer is the stress type of the Loyal Skeptic and the Loyal Skeptic is the security type of the Performer. Both types share a pleasant, people pleasing personality although Performers tend to be more secure and trusting when they move towards sixes while Loyal Skeptics in stress become more active and eager to meet their goals. On the positive side, when a Performer moves towards six, they become more familial and group oriented as well as vulnerable and emotionally accessible (in a good way). On the negative side, they can be more fearful of rejection, and more anxious and indecisive.

Mediator 9 (stress type): On the positive side, when a Performer moves towards 9, they can be more relaxed and peaceful and receptive. They can gain a better perspective on life. On the negative side, when a Performer moves towards 9, they can procrastinate, become apathetic and neglect themselves to the point of serious harm.

Overlaps between the Performer and other non-connected types

The Perfectionist 1: These two types both place a high value on goal-oriented activities and share a tendency to place work above all else. However, whereas the Perfectionist suffers because of a harsh inner critic, the Performer might look for short cuts in order to get ahead.

The Epicure 7: The similarities between these types derive from the fact that both are active and energetic—and often too busy. Both love to avoid negative feelings, including sadness. Their main difference comes from the fact that while Epicures feel entitled to their own wellbeing, Performers are driven by a sense of social approval. Performers are interested in being efficient, while Epicures care more for pleasure.

The Protector 8: Performers and Protectors are similar because both are assertive and action-oriented. Both are natural leaders who are not afraid to step on someone who gets in their way. The main difference is that while Protectors can be confrontational and attached to their position, Performers can be angered when someone gets in the way of their achievement.

Chapter 11: Ennea-Type Three – "The Achiever"

Aliases: The Performer, The Motivator

The Pragmatic, Success-Oriented type.

Generally described as:

Adaptable   Outstanding
Image-ConsciousDriven

At their best, Type Three people are described as:

AuthenticRole Model

EnthusiasticInspirational

Motto: "I need to succeed. Get to the top and look good doing it!"

The Achiever in General

People who exhibit a Core Type Three have a strong desire to look good to other people, because they are motivated by gaining love and acceptance through their achievements and performance. They strive to be outstanding – to stand out.

Type Three people genuinely want the approval and admiration of those around them, and they pour their energy into performing to others' satisfaction.

They are graceful and gracious, and easily accomplish things that others admire. Achievers sometimes equate their self-worth with their performance, and can defer to others' desires, ultimately repressing or deceiving themselves about their true wants.

When a Type Three person can fully engage and express themselves, they become shining stars; they light up any room. They enjoy inspiring and lifting others, pushing themselves and those around them to new limits. They make charming company, excellent hosts and social mediators, and become a positive force, pushing others to achieve their own hopes and dreams.

Sometimes, while a Type Three person works toward their goals, they can become single-minded and cut-throat, even disregarding the harm they do others. They greatly fear failure and rejection and work both to be successful and to seem successful. Achievers prefer to be seen as "winners," thinking of themselves as "the best" at whatever they set their minds to. This can make them open to connecting with others they see as winners, or it can make them competitive and closed off from relationships with others who can steal their spotlight.

When a Type Three person develops their social status and reputation to the extent that they receive the attention and encouragement they crave, they feel fulfilled. Type Three people are satisfied by appreciation, not the material "things" associated with success. Being seen as a star makes an Achiever feel worthwhile, which in turn drives them to encourage others to shine.

How Achievers See Themselves vs. How Others See Them

Achievers see themselves as true leaders, modeling the road to success for others to follow, but they can become narrow-minded, intense, and relentless in their pursuits. They think they are driven by a true desire to stand out – highly exceptional – but actually, Achievers generally operate under fears of being ordinary, bored, and rejected. They seek reassurance from others that their efforts and actions make them special. While the Achiever believes they are competent and deserve praise, other people may see their confidence as arrogance or snobbery.

Achievers are highly invested in seeing themselves as worthy – worthy of love, of admiration, of praise, of followers – sometimes despite their competitive nature, which can push others away. When they think others don't recognize their achievements, they may work harder and perform more dramatically.

Because Type Three people are so in-tune with the wants, needs, and preferences of others, they may resort to dishonesty to boost their reputation. They prefer to think of themselves as deeply empathetic, but others may see Achievers as insensitive. While they notice and can react to other people's emotions, they don't spend much time in their own emotional landscape. When they ignore their own feelings for too long, they have trouble connecting with their true desires. This disconnect can make them angry, which they may redirect to people close to them, blaming others for "making" them work so hard.

The "Average" Achiever's Mental Health

When an Achiever is at an average level of health, they may feel naturally self-conscious and adjust themselves to meet others' expectations. They will be efficient in solving problems, thinking them through, but can lose their true desires in the process. Sometimes demanding and overbearing, Achievers at this level tend to "act out" for attention, while also downplaying their dramatic nature and single-mindedness.

When an Achiever feels a little better, they may be performing well and achieving their goals regularly, which fuels their drive to push themselves further. At this level of health, an Achiever wants to be recognized and works hard to earn that recognition, although others may become frustrated by their focus and drive.

Moving Toward Integration: Achievers At Their Best

When moving in their Direction of Integration (growth) and exhibiting their best qualities, Achievers become supportive and enthusiastic for others' achievements. As they achieve, they become less vain and self-centered.

Basic Desire(s): To feel valuable and worthwhile.

Basic Motivation(s): To be affirmed and recognized, to be distinguished from others and admired, and to impress others.

Unique Gift(s): Positive, confident, and optimistic; always able to see the glass as half-full.

Basic Goal: To be successful, productive, and accepted.

When Achiever's Mental Health is Excellent

When at their best, Achievers are genuinely generous, charming, and warmly inclusive. They can channel their drive to succeed into support for others and enjoy the accomplishments of people they support. Motivating to others, confident and caring, Type Three people embody an easy, graceful way of living that laughs loud and often. When motivated by their own achievements, they naturally elevate those around them.

As Type Three people Disintegrate, they become focused on being liked and accepted and less inclined to rely on their inner sources of confidence. Seeking the approval and acknowledgement of the group, they begin to disregard the feelings of people close to them, as they become more self-centered in their focus on achieving.

Moving Toward Disintegration: Achievers When Stressed

When moving in their Direction of Disintegration (stress), the normally ambitious and confident Achiever regresses toward becoming competitive and self-centered.

Basic Fear(s): Afraid of rejection, failure, and social outcast.
Triggering Emotion: Deceit

Becomes Fixated On: **Vanity**

Outwardly focused Type Three people become apathetic and defensive under stress. Confused about their true feelings, or afraid to admit them for fear of "disappointing" others, Achievers fall prey to their self-doubts when they feel ignored. They can begin to lie to themselves and others about what they really want, and they become needy, potentially manipulative or vengeful. Most of all, they cry out for positive attention. When an Achiever can't receive recognition for their successes, they will settle for whatever gets them attention.

What Type Three People Might Struggle With

Type Three people suffer from suppressing emotions, setting aside their true desires to align with the goals of the group. Disconnecting from their authentic wants can make them lonely, even in the middle of a crowd.

At times, Type Threes can become dramatic in their search for attention, or competitive as they become frustrated when they see achievements they believe they deserve being earned by others. A Type Three person might struggle with showing their support or genuinely celebrating other people's victories, although they expect others to congratulate them on their accomplishments.

Type Threes tend to push themselves to their physical, mental, and emotional breaking points. Their expectations of themselves are high, and they can be relentlessly critical of themselves in their pursuit of excellence.

When Achiever's Mental Health is Struggling

When fully disintegrated and under stress, Achievers become vengeful, merciless in the pursuit of their goals. They can fixate on their jealousy of others' successes, even working to undermine that success. The Achiever might even excuse their insensitive actions toward others as "the ends justify the means," because they are so intensely driven to reach those ends.

As Achievers decrease their stress and focus on their health, they can reveal their inner vulnerabilities — fear of failure and humiliation. The healthy Achiever's mindset recognizes that working collectively is a path to success that can fulfill them, giving them joy they can't experience through achievements earned alone.

Potential Addictive Struggles

Type Three people might struggle with addictions associated with their ideas of success. An Achiever whose goals are physical can overwork or overstress their body, exhausting or injuring themselves and placing their physical health at risk. An Achiever whose success is defined by their professional work may overwork themselves with heavy job responsibilities, long hours, and minimal breaks or recovery time.

Some Type Three people may struggle with addictions to substances that "fuel" their desires to work long hours, push their body physically, or give off the appearance of a successful lifestyle. Caffeine, amphetamines, cocaine, steroids, or other stimulants are common addictive struggles for Achievers.

Overcoming Challenges of the Achiever Ennea-Type

Achievers must give themselves time to recharge. Honestly connecting with their inner needs is essential, because they may spend so much time performing for others that they forget themselves. Practicing self-appreciation, integrating small breaks into the day, and genuinely connecting with others helps the Achiever stay balanced and at their best.

Being the Best Achiever

Harness the best aspects of your Achiever Ennea-type and diminish negative traits that emerge under stress. If you're an Achiever, or know someone who is, consider using the following techniques to help you unlock and grow the best version of yourself.

Truthful Reflection

Type Three people need to "stop and smell the roses." They are focused and driven, and they can drive themselves to exhaustion. To maintain balance, an Achiever can take a short break – even a few deep breaths can do it – to pause during busy or stressful times. Use these moments to reconnect with true inner desires, which tend to get lost during the bustle of impressing others. Achievers can have difficulty letting go of their goals, but learning to congratulate themselves on small achievements can realign an Achiever with their next goal.

Suggestions:

Goal-oriented journaling. Meditate. Practice yoga. Keep a success chart. Scrapbooking. Garden. Bake. Clean. Keep a "To-Do" list and update when items are completed.

Develop Social Bonds

Type Three people naturally love to be around others, and when they refine their communication and bonding skills, they encourage everyone around them to achieve. The Achiever at their best finds joy in projects that don't advance them toward their own goals, but instead support the goals of others. Enhancing cooperative abilities can establish the Achiever as an appreciated, beloved leader in their community.

Achievers can become frustrated when it seems that others aren't as dedicated to the project, or when they believe they're not receiving appropriate recognition. Learning to take pride in themselves, and express their pride in others' achievements, will help the Achiever feel loved and fulfilled.

Suggestions

Take on a mentoring or teaching role. Converse with a nonjudgmental, supportive friend. Start a podcast or blog. Join an online or offline community of like-minded people. Practice active listening. Choose one time each day to contact someone you know and tell them you appreciate them. Say "thank you" at the end of every conversation.

There are simple things an Achiever can do to release their deep appreciation for talent, beauty, and leadership, especially when they give themselves permission to praise themselves and others.

Chapter 12: Personal Growth Through

The Enneagram

Have you ever spent hours on a jigsaw puzzle only to realize that a key piece is missing? Your first response is probably: "It can't be missing. It must be here somewhere." You pick up every available piece in turn. You search under the table and across the floor. You run your fingers over the completed parts of the puzzle, hoping your fingers will see something your eyes have missed.

You can walk away from a jigsaw puzzle that is missing a piece. It is harder to walk away from the hope that your life will come together in a meaningful whole. The Enneagram is a system for thinking about human personality and motivation that helps people understand the patterns in their own lives and the lives of people around them. Many people use the

Enneagram to discover the piece they were afraid they were missing.

Based on a combination of ancient wisdom and modern social science, the Enneagram is a model that describes the patterns people typically use to motivate themselves, relate to others and face threats or obstacles. The centre of the system is the recognition that the strategies that work best for us eventually also become the fault lines that leave us vulnerable. We do not always have strengths and weaknesses: sometimes the same quality is both a strength and a weakness.

It is one thing to overcome your faults. It is another thing entirely to overcome your strengths. The Enneagram will describe you in terms of what you want most, what you fear most, and what you are likely to do to achieve results you like. It is dynamic in the way that human beings are dynamic; the Enneagram describes how we change when we feel secure or stressed, and how we move between different selves in different contexts. A circle with nine points, the Enneagram describes all of us as part of one whole, a human family in which we are all connected and related.

The most powerful ways to use the Enneagram is for deepening your relationships with others. I believe that understanding others on a deeper level can help you to work, live, or love them better. The Enneagram will give your insight into what makes someone tick, and often gives perspective which can propel your relationship beyond most interpersonal issues. This information is held in such high esteem, it is currently being used by therapists, life coaches, and in business to create more dynamic and efficient teams. This is not your average typeing system or hocus pocus.

All of my relationships have changed since I began studying the Enneagram. Most have gotten much better, some of just changed, and some I've decided to end because they weren't serving the purpose they were meant to. Based on the experience I had with understanding others through the Enneagram, I'm going to show you the four steps you can use to understand friends, family, and colleagues better.

4 Steps to Better Relationships Through the Enneagram:

Determine your own type and the type of the person whom you wish to understand better.

It is my hope that you know your type already and at least have some understanding of the Enneagram. If not, I would suggest looking at an overview of the Enneagram and the nine types. You should get yourself acquainted with the nine types and your own type before you attempt to understand someone else better. As with most types of personal development... an ounce of self-understanding is a pound of understanding others.

If you are truly stumped with finding your own type, I would suggest trying a free Enneagram type test. These are not 100% perfect, but they can usually peg someone to one or two types and you can take it from there.

Look at the fears and desires & key motivations of the type you are hoping to understand more.

On Wikipedia, you can take a close look at the fears and desires of the type you are looking to understand more. For instance, if that person happened to be an Enneagram Type 7, their fears and desires would look like this:

"Basic Fear: Of being deprived and in pain

Basic Desire: To be satisfied and content-- to have their needs fulfilled

Key Motivations: Want to maintain their freedom and happiness, to avoid missing out on worthwhile experiences, to keep themselves excited and occupied, to avoid and discharge pain."

Taking a close look at this will give you some insight into a problem you might be having or a way to avoid future problems. Enneagram Type 7's are infamous for being afraid they are going to be left out of the fun or stuck in a boring place without a way out. That may seem a little dramatic, of course, but it's true. So, if you are an office manager, it would be unlikely that your office's Enneagram Type 7 would be the best person to man the phones all day. The seven would be more suited to be out on sales calls or mowing the lawn. Think excitement, short attention span, not really an anchor. (Dear 7's, don't take this personally, I'm a 7 too...)

Look at your type compatibility.

The Enneagram Institute offers a great type compatibility chart. Google "Enneagram Institute Type Compatibility Chart" and head on over. You can select your own type and the type you are looking to understand better. To continue with our example from above: Let's assume that the office manager is a type 3 and the worker is still a type 7, here is a part of the compatibility report:

"This is a highly complementary pair: both types are self-assertive, have high energy, and are outgoing and capable of being around people with relative ease. Both types bring optimism, a future orientation, the sense of possibility and renewal to their relationships and to enterprises they become involved with. Threes can work alone more easily than Sevens, although both are stimulated by interacting with people and both can be excellent communicators of their ideas and values. Both are persuasive and articulate, often lively and attractive, making them sought after company. Both have a youthful orientation such that they feed off of each other's energy: no other couple is as vivacious or gregarious as the Three/Seven couple. This is probably the highest energy combination of types and they wholeheartedly engage in lots of activities, plans and projects, with the emphasis on attaining the good life. The focus is on sociability, going out, having adventures together and on realizing possibilities and on finding personal fulfillment. "

Use this for good only, not evil.

Once you get a grasp on all of this, you have a lot of inside information into people's motivations. You also get a lot of perspective on how you work with others. It's a lot of responsibility. Don't go abusing your power and manipulating situations. Be good, and the study of the Enneagram can bring a lot of clarity and peace to your relationships.

STEPS TO BETTER RELATIONSHIPS THROUGH THE ENNEAGRAM

One of the most powerful ways to use the Enneagram is for deepening your relationships with others. I believe that understanding others on a deeper level can help you to work, live, or love them better. The Enneagram will give you insight into what makes someone tick, and often gives perspective which can propel your relationship beyond most interpersonal issues. This information is held in such high esteem, it is currently being used by therapists, life coaches, and in business to create more dynamic and efficient teams. This is not your average typeing system or hocus pocus.

All of my relationships have changed since I began studying the Enneagram. Most have gotten much better, some of just changed, and some I've decided to end because they weren't serving the purpose they were meant to. Based on the experience I had with understanding others through the Enneagram, I'm going to show you the four steps you can use to understand friends, family, and colleagues better.

Subtypes In The Enneagram: Why They Matter

Types form the foundation of enneagram trance but there are a number of other factors that help to articulate individuals within types. One of these categories is that of "sub-types". Subtypes are lie proverbial three legged stools. Usually there will be one leg that is the strongest in a person's ego state, followed by a second subtype that the person also embraces to a lesser degree. The third leg will be missing for most people. This missing piece is largely the cause of imbalance within the ego state. Consider these three subtypes:

Self-preservation- These people are typically concerned primarily with their own safety and that of those around them. They are the people who are stocking up for Y2K and keeping back stocks of basic supplies both in their cars and in their homes. Preparation, regardless of their basic type, is a hallmark of these subtypes.

Sexual or One to one-- These people prefer one to one contacts and conversations and interactions. While they can function in social groups, they will tend to seek out individuals within groups for much of their connection. Their preference gives them an intensity that sets them apart from the other two subtypes.

Herd Instinct -- These people are joiners. They get their identity largely from what they associate with. They are the people who love sports teams, political parties, brand name clothing and other associations with others. Being an individual is not as important to them as their affiliations with group identities and following the crowd.

Subtypes are extremely useful in understanding our own preferences in social interaction and the particular intensity that we bring to situations. When we're working to understand our own types or those of people around us, it's vitally important to consider subtypes, both the primary and the secondary types, as well as the third one that is being rejected as unimportant. For example, someone who has little or no herd instinct will appear highly individualistic and likely have trouble bonding in identity in groups or networking with groups. This can be a handicap in professional/career development in some professions. Those who have trouble in one to one interactions will find it more difficult to interview, to sustain intimate relations with one to one subtype people and sometimes can appear to lack certain depth in conversational skills. Those who lack self preservation may have trouble understanding when danger or the need for self protection is truly present, retaining little or nothing that they might need for their very real safety.

The enneagram is not a simple '9 types fit all' system. There are a number of elements that go into understanding trance. Subtypes are all part of the subtle color variations that we see in the nine types and need to be considered as we look at ourselves and others in their daily functioning.

The Enneagram is an ancient tool of uncertain origin, said to be brought in by real genies some how. Also called the Sufi numbers is like the chess board game and some other things of amazing design that have always been around.

The Enneagram is an outline of the nine basic personality types; it shows the advantages and limitations of every intelligent being born in this planet.

The outline of the nine personality types, with a modern interpretation is as follows.

The Perfectionist, The number one is a much disciplined person, wants the best quality at any price. They make pretty good villain characters in movies because they are very unconcerned with human suffering, they are the perfect inquisitor.

The Server, also known as the Helper, or the Saint. They are usually very service oriented people, helping every one. Sometimes they become intrusive manipulators, that want others to do what they want because they feel it is the only right and good way to do it in the Universe. A classic is the beggar that yells at people.

The chameleon, also known as climber. This guy is nice and all gifted, but his niceness is just apparent. You can see them changing before your eyes and turning against you as a crisis emerges. Nobody can usually believe that they are fake personalities, because they build a nice smile and an outlook of a good character while in reality they are kind of divorced from their true feelings.

The extra sensitive is an artist like personality. Tends to depression and envy of what others have done with their lives. Some suicidal tendencies are possible, because he is aware of his own impulses at the same time that feels guilty about it. For others it may seem as if such a person exaggerates in her emotional concerns about other peoples reactions.

The paranoid nerd. This guy is very intellectual, but at the same time, he gets distracted. He sees logical connections in everything. He always wants to know the right explanation for the relevant phenomena that occur everywhere. He may get paranoid and build conspiracy theories and cure all remedies. He likes recognition for his brilliant mind and also wants to find a way to fit in the word he sees around as somehow frightening.

The devils advocate. He can be a loyal follower or a bad seditious gossiper enemy. Inside he has a lot of tension that he relieves by finding the worst interpretation possible for others peoples behavior, and telling everyone what his twisted mind thinks. He assumes everybody else to be the worst, except the one that he is loyal to. He may look like an unconcerned bastard, but he is a very dutiful hard worker and a masochistic character.

The maniac. This guy is peter pan, he never grows up. He is always an immature child. He yells and fights for things and items that he needs so badly that it is even scary. It could be food, videogames, a ticket for the theater, you name it. He is selfish and not too often concerned about sharing the goods evenly.

The tyrant dictator. He could also make a great boss or leader. He has a very powerful personality, always grounded in the bottom line. When he is unbalanced he may act as a mafia chief, threatening everybody who doesn't accommodate to his desires. In the positive side he could be a true hero and philanthropist.

The nine is the most unavailable person in the planet. A peacemaker kind of alienated unconscious person that lives in a perpetual quiet disconnection. He or she may go with you to a party, and then forget completely that you are there.

Sometimes they have awakenings like, Oh my but you have been here all this time!

The Enneagram is in reality a Master tool for transformations, used by group dynamics trainers to create transformational exercises, touching every aspect of the human shadow limitations pool, with the intention to overcome it. It creates the most tremendous breakthroughs in shadow master transformations and it has been a matter for very serious studies.

Chapter 13: Enneagram Type 7

In this section, you will see eight good qualities, eight stressors, and eight stress behaviors of enneagram Type 7.

Mark with a tick which ones apply to you.

GOOD QUALITIES

7s like to have fun and they appear upbeat as the most joyful type of the Enneagram. They are upbeat, optimistic and adventurous. What is important is to 7s is to have fun, and experience as much of life as possible. They love to try new things and travel broadly to find new sources of endless excitement. They are often the life of the party, and where they go, the sunshine follows.

7s have an enthusiastic and optimistic outlook on life. Like the colors of the rainbow, there is always something interesting to do in life. They are resourceful in coming up with something new, and creative to occupy themselves with, and you can always find them enjoying the many pleasures of life. 7s always seem to have a way in which they can spice up their lives, and inject something new and playful into their surroundings.

7s have a natural charm and this makes them charismatic individuals. If you ask them how they are doing, they would reply: 'I couldn't be better.' They put on a happy face and carry with them comedy, jokes, smiles, and laughter. 7s are engaging, fond of company, and talkative. They are easily fascinated by their own ideas, and in turn, other people are captivated by their charisma.

7s are the eternal child and they experience life like a gift. They are constantly playing, and when they are not, they are mentally engaged in planning for the next great adventure, and where the biggest fireworks in life are to be found. They always have youthful energy about them. They express a childlike astonishment, and that makes them love having fun, the way kids do.

7s are visionary people who often have a grand plan for the future. They dream big and are full of hope of how the world can be a better, happier, and more pleasurable place. They are fascinated by the future possibilities and love imagining what life there would be like. For 7s, life is a Disneyland, full of miracles and surprises just waiting to happen. In their mind, they can see a better tomorrow, and that makes them love brainstorming and coming up with creative ideas as solutions to a problem.

Many 7s are inspirational people, and they speak in a highly enthusiastic and exuberant manner. With their positive outlook, they have the ability to lift people's spirits up and they make excellent storytellers. They also engage in motivational speaking, they are natural communicators and they take to the stage well. With their light-hearted and funny anecdotes, they enjoy entertaining people and seeing others smile and laugh with them.

7s have a bright, bubbly spirit and rarely allow themselves to get down and depressed. They bounce right back up like colorful helium balloons. 7s believe that 'Life is beautiful'. And if their present environment doesn't offer anything fascinating for them, they can easily retreat to the pleasures of their mind, of which there are no restrictions.

7s are multi-talented and have a wide range of interests. With their quick and agile mind, they can learn new skills with little effort. Whether it is a new sport, a musical instrument, dance or a new job, 7s try everything enjoyable in life and are the modern renaissance person.

STRESSORS

7s are overburdened by needing to be upbeat and optimistic. They believe if they are not happy and joyful they will not be loved. When the world of a 7 is not as it should be, here is what can pop into their minds.

"I have to stay upbeat and optimistic"

"I'm held back from having fun"

"I can't be sad or depressed"

"I must avoid pain and suffering or I won't survive"

"I am bored and uninspired"

"This is too routine and limiting"

"I am starting to get dragged down"

"I am trapped and restricted"

STRESS BEHAVIORS

Some of the behaviors 7s exhibit under stress is as follows.

7s attention becomes distracted and scattered over a range of activities. Because they are very sensitive to pain, depression, and hurt, their mind scatters to avoid these things. Their energy is driven in many directions at the same time and they remain unable to focus on the task in hand.

7s need to stay excited and they plan and anticipate more. They reflect on a pleasurable moment in the past or dream up new ideas of pleasure in the future. They move quickly and can appear to know many things. But when they share their thoughts they act entitled to recognition and support even though what they say may lack substance and depth.

7s will avoid being pinned down and escape from boredom, pain, and suffering. They panic and run away from routine tasks or relationships that are no longer fun to them. They are oblivious to the suffering in others, as whenever they feel down, they will get up, put their best clothes on, and go out dancing.

7s are interested in many things but may not pursue any of them in-depth and end up becoming dilettante and superficial. They sample a lot of goods but don't relish, assimilate them, or spend time going through things in depth. They do not commit to seeing through any of their projects to completion and have a long string of starts but no finishes.

Keeping up momentum is important to a 7 so they can act impulsively, coming up with fanciful ideas on a whim, and leaping before they look. Once they come up with an idea they can also be intensely demanding and pushy to get others to go along with their plans.

7s love a variety of options and keep their options open right until the last minute. They cannot decide on which outcome would give them the most pleasure and do not want to give up a good option and end up deprived. They become unable to stick to any commitments for fear of being stuck or trapped. They flip-flop from one idea to the next, and as a result, their good ideas never come to fruition.

7s have an insatiable appetite for pleasure, and want instant gratification, distracting themselves with pleasurable options. They become gluttonous and overindulgent. Nothing is moving fast enough or meets their needs quickly enough. They will not listen to others as they want to experience as many things as possible to find out for themselves what will satisfy them.

7s become hedonistic and excessive. They want to have it all or try it all. They live life in the fast lane, are lavish with money and spending, and can become addicted to excitement. The more experiences they have, the more they want, and they go from one hit and high to the next. Partying hard, and staying up and having fun all night. Even sleep is too boring for many 7s.

TEST RESULTS

Here's how you interpret your Enneagram Test Results.

Scoring (one point for each tick):

Good qualities: 0 – 8

Stressors: 0 -8 (divide by 2)

Stress behaviors: 0 - 8

Divide your stressors score by 2, and add to your good qualities and stress behaviors scores for a total of 0 - 20.

A result of **12 or more** means you identify strongly with the Enneagram Type 7. It could either be your core type (7), your wing (6,8), or you could be connected to the type by a line (1,4,5).

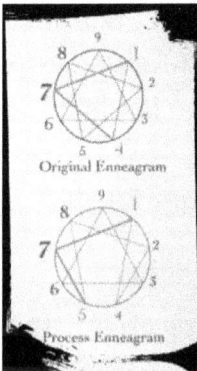

Original Enneagram

Process Enneagram

Chapter 14: The Point Eight Archetype :

The Challenger

Challengers are a body-based enneagram personality type who are known for their sheer intensity. They know who they are, and they know what needs to be done – and they will let you know what they need you to do. If there is ever a personality type that people can allude to when they speak of "born leaders", it's the Challenger. They're the type who can compel others to follow them anywhere.

Identifying A Challenger

Challengers are assertive and forceful. They have this energy that is so intense , it's almost angry. They tend to reflect the power of "something higher", be that their god, their moral code, their vision of how things should be. Think Martin Luther King Jr and Winston Churchill. They can galvanize an entire people. They want to see a world that is more just and they encourage other people to stand up for what's right. You can see them leading the world – from households, to classrooms, businesses, and military organizations.

However, they can come on too strong or become confrontational. They struggle with keeping their tempers in check and in showing vulnerability. Unhealthy Eights can be egocentric and domineering. Eights who are not stable can have quick temper and can become violent when provoked. At worst, they can become bullies who revel in seeing other people cower in their presence. Healthy ones, however are masters of their own selves. They are in control but they use their power to help other people. They are high-minded and even heroic.

Dominant Traits

Charismatic – Eights inspire action because their passion draws other people to their cause. They speak in a dramatic and forceful way. That's why they're the kind who can drive tremendous change not just in their circle but in the whole world.

Tenacious – Challengers have tremendous amounts of mental and physical endurance. However, they tend to neglect their own health and wellbeing.

Fair – Eights have a solid sense of justice. They will make sure that everyone gets their due. They don't play favorites.

Independent – Eights do not care what other people think. They enjoy being self-reliant and they have very solid assessments of the way things are and how things should be. They are fully behind the mindset that "if you want to get something done, you have to do it yourself". If they absolutely have to collaborate people, they want to be in a position of leadership.

Protective –. They will stand up for other people, be it subordinates, friends, family, or just another human being. They will not take anything sitting down.

Resourceful – Challengers like figuring out how to accomplish things and will do everything in their power to get things done. They are constantly on the lookout for situations in which they could test their mettle in order to showcase their power and superiority.

Straightforward – Eights have the ability to convey their message, which is one of the reasons that they can inspire action.

Thinking Patterns

Eights enjoy taking on challenges, hence the name, but they also love empowering other people to challenge themselves and become better. They are strong-willed and persistent, but they also encourage others to be that way.

They are more than willing to defy the status quo especially if they perceive an injustice. They're not afraid; it doesn't matter who or what they're fighting, and what the public will think of them. However, unhealthy challengers could end up doing things to break social norms just to show that they're the ones in control.

Eights have little tolerance for weakness, be it physical or emotional, and while they do have strong feelings for justice they might not be able to show much sympathy. In fact, they can seem inconsiderate.

When an eight enters a room, he will assess his surroundings and look for opportunities to show their importance. They have power and they'd like you to know that.

Eights likes being in charge. They don't let others have power over them, be it physical, psychological, sexual, financial, or social.

They absolutely refuse to be indebted to anyone or to comply with social conventions.

Core Fears

The eight's core fear is rejection. If they sense a looming rejection, such as a breakup, or getting fired, they will become hostile in attempt to regain control. They would want to feel like it is their choice to end the relationship or to quit.

Eights are scared of not being in control for fear of being emotionally harmed. They are afraid of being vulnerable, which is why they have the tendency to push away the people who love them. At worst, they can be controlling and aggressive in an attempt to maintain emotional distance. They do have a sentimental side but it's buried deep inside them.

Core Desires

Eights want to be in control of their own selves. They want to be completely self-reliant and they're always looking out to show strength and resist weakness. They also want to be the dominant force in their environment – they want to be important and in control.

What Eights Need To Work On

Eights prioritize justice above all. However, they can

Eights have difficulty paying any attention to what other people have to say. If you're an eight, be mindful of this tendency and try to be more open. You won't always get hurt if you listen. And sometimes, the best decision is not your decision. You never know what other people can say that could solve a problem.

Challengers could also be so domineering and assertive that they forget one important thing – empathy. Sometimes, they get so focused on how things should be done that they neglect to think about what other people feel. Be on the lookout for such scenarios and remind yourself to be gentle – or at least have mercy.

Be careful not to overvalue power be it in the form of wealth, position, or physical strength. Just because you can does not mean you should. Otherwise, you run the risk of having people in your life that do not really love or respect you – they just fear you.

Challenges That Eights Usually Face

Eights may have a problem connecting with other people because they do not want to be vulnerable. That's why they have a tendency to be perceived as unapproachable, when the truth is, they can be quite the protective and reliable friend.

They can even go as far as rejecting others outright because they do not want to be the ones to get rejected.

They may have a tendency to disregard other people's suggestions and opinions.

They have a problem recognizing authority and find it difficult to follow rules.

Unhealthy eights can go as far as inflicting physical harm, so it's important you are aware of how balanced you are.

Challengers and Relationships

In terms of professional settings, Eights tend to take charge of situations. That's why they usually have leadership roles, and they're good at it. They get things done. They are not at all passive.

Healthy eights are honorable. In the workplace, they will take the heat when needed. They understand they have to make tough decisions and they can't please everyone. However, they will always lookout for the interests of their subordinates.

When Eights do determine you to be trustworthy, you will be welcomed into their inner circle and you will have a reliable and loyal friend. They are magnanimous to their friends and they will stand up for you when needed.

The very things that help make Eights such a strong precursor of change – their strong will, self-mastery, tough-mindedness, and confidence can result to problems developing intimate relationships if they are not cognizant enough and have the propensity to deny weakness. They want to appear in control so they will erect walls and refuse to lower their defenses.

Eights can be clueless when it comes to personal relationships. They are so hardworking that they may end up losing emotional contact with their partners or friends, which does not make sense for eights. For example, they wouldn't understand why their family seems to be unhappy that they don't get to spend quality time together when they're doing their best to work hard.

Eights may lash out when they're vulnerable and because they have quick tempers, they can explode quickly. However, they do forget their anger quickly as well.

Career Options For Challengers

Eights are known for their fairness, logical decision making and ability to express themselves clearly in almost every situation. They are highly individualistic and courageous. Those are some of the reasons that they make great lawyers, judges, company directors, and business owners. Their charisma and capacity to inspire others to action makes them good politicians. Eights will also make good fundraisers, and urban planners because they can take a sustainable approach in which a community's needs are met while the environment is protected.

How To Interact With An Eight

Avoid pussyfooting. Challengers hate double speak and mind games. So if you have something to say, be direct.

Be calm and steady when calling out an Eight's violent behavior.

Avoid harping on them with their vulnerabilities. If you have to give constructive feedback, do so in between positive comments.

Let them know you appreciate their protection. But when they do become controlling, don't shun them. Talk to them calmly and clearly about how you're feeling .

Eights put so many walls up that they can smell manipulation from a mile away. So if you want something, put all your cards on the table. Be straightforward

Eights are averse to uncertainty so be as clear as possible when communicating. They could entirely withdraw from contact if they encounter vagueness.

Debating with an Eight about morality is futile. They have a solid sense of justice.

How To Be Your Best Self As An Eight

Be mindful. Observe the impact of your words (including those you use in self-talk) and actions. And actively practice empathy – including for yourself. Remember that compassion is not a weakness.

Know that you are loved (or can be loved – just make it easy for the people in your life). It doesn't have to be you against the world.

Be okay with accepting help from others. It's not a sign of weakness. Interdependency helps relationships grow. In fact, it's human nature to feel affinity to those they see as someone that they can help. People like to feel that they are needed.

Recognize that no one is invulnerable. You can, however, work on your weaknesses so you can deal with situations better. It's in knowing your weaknesses that you know which areas you can improve on. You can't improve if you don't realize and acknowledge that improvement is needed.

Use force wisely. It's true that you wield power, but before you use brute force, think about whether the situation really needs it.

Listen to other people. Be introspective even when you feel that your authority is being questioned. Evaluate whether that is truly the case or if the other person is merely trying to suggest something. Sometimes, it's best to yield to those who can execute something better than you can. Everyone has a specialty. There are many things you are knowledgeable at but you can't do and know everything. No one can, and that's okay.

Chapter 15: The Enneagram And Spiritual

Practice

The Spiritual Journey

Ian Cron said, "Insight is cheap." What uses has insight if it is not used for the greater good of transformation, improvement, and growth. At the end of the day, you want to use the enneagram to enhance your spiritual development. You want to become a better person.

The point of focus for working on yourself is to turn to God. You should always endeavor to turn to God to heal your soul and become the best version of yourself. Depending on any tool other than God can be idolatry. As a Christian, you don't want to depend on anything rather than the finished work of Christ to become a better person.

It is also very important to understand that changing the deeply rooted habits, behaviors and ways of life that have been ingrained in us through childhood takes time. It can't be removed in just a few minutes. Cleaning the subconscious mind and ridding it from all kind deadly sins takes time and patience. Leaning on God is critical in this respect.

Without the Enneagram, you might be unconsciously exhibiting or committing the deadly sins of your personality type. For example, a type one might just be expecting other people to be perfect in a certain way. He might be highly critical when things don't look right, good or perfect. You might not understand why you exhibit this type of "self-righteous anger."

But the knowledge of the Enneagram will shed light on this aspect of your personality. Once you discover your blind spots, you should consider how to work on yourself. If you are in a relationship or marriage, you might want to examine how your perfect driven emotional drive has caused problems in your marriage.

Find ways to be more patient and understanding with people. Find ways to make allowances for people and understand them from their point of view. Examine your life, could it be that the same thing that you are criticizing your partner for you are also a victim of it?

If you are type 8 who loves giving, you might want to watch your hidden motives for giving and extending a helping hand to others. Is it to please people? Is to get others approval? Is to win other people's favor? Is it to make yourself known? Is it to get attention? Is it to get respect from others? Is it to impress people?

Even though it is good to give, you have to make sure that you are giving with pure motives. You might use the enneagram to begin your "inner work". Start working on yourself and removing any proud, the arrogant, boastful and impressive motive behind your acts of giving. Learn to give cheerfully without any form of pride behind it. In this way, the Enneagram can be used as powerful for personal and spiritual transformation.

Chapter 16: How The Enneagram Can Actually Improve Your Life And Make You Really Happier

The Enneagram is an antiquated character frame that could uncover a part of your hidden wants and anxieties. Something which the enneagram can notify you to see yourself is that you're so frantic to find something which seems to be almost unattainable. This will explore some of the things which each enneagram type looks for during everyday life, except finds hard actually to maintain or manage.

This is exactly what You Desperately Crave in Life, According to Your Enneagram Type

Enneagram 1

A person, you enormously need a sense of respectability and wholeness within yourself. You may generally be a fussbudget, and once in a while, it may feel like there is a judge sitting within your cerebrum getting from the entirety of your disappointments and the remainder of the people around you. You continue expecting you can arrive at your best, accomplish that aim, or crush all the "awful" parts of yourself. Sometimes it seems like about the off possibility which you're able to keep on investing enough effort in the future that belief of wholeness and stability is going to appear. You will, at last, have the choice to rest knowing you've vanquished your bad presence. Have you ever arrived at this time, or would you really feel like it is a goal you won't ever reach?

What to Do:

Sensing That you will need to at all times attempt to "virtue," the presence you have been awarded will consume out you and contribute to nervousness and endless disappointment. Yet much as may be anticipated, try to generate harmony with the various sides of yourself light and dimness. Everybody has a fuzzy side.

Attempt not to dismiss what seems to be right or incorrect to you, but do not harp on previous mistakes or disappointments. Excuse yourself to the wrongs you have completed and pardon the others on the off possibility which you may. Have a gander on your own with compassion for a change and floor yourself now. What would you have the ability to do today that's astute yet kind to yourself as well as some other men and women? What are your ardent and physiological needs at the current moment? Maybe what is best would be just to allow yourself to sit together with your possessions and shortcomings for a while. Have a gander at yourself really however, with compassion. Know yourself, both the colourful components as well as the helpless pieces. This will let you be even more whole inside and not as split and disappointed.

Enneagram 2

I have always wanted a sense of experiencing a location, solidarity, and enjoy. You may generally place other people's requirements facing your own, and you're ordinarily liberal and warm. You live to create beneficial things happen for people, yet that which you ache for is getting this affection provided right back to you. You have to feel confessed, confessed, and verified. You worry that without giving away yourself, you a few manners or another are unworthy. You think you want to secure enjoyment through magnanimity, agreeableness, and penance. Some of this time this leads one to be employee hearted and sympathetic; distinct events this may lead you to become exhausted, worn out, and mad.

What to Do:

You may fall into the trap of having things done for people with an end goal to obtain confirmation and insistence consequently. Have a gander in your intentions behind attaining something before you merely proceed to assist different men and women. It's safe to state that you're doing so because you genuinely care about their prosperity? Can it be much better compared to the off possibility they handled this issue? Or on the flip side, could you say you're doing this so that you may find some type of sense of value back in return? Be quite legit with yourself regarding your thought processes, tune into your own heart, your mind, and your physique. It's safe to state that you're overlooking your own requirements, both enthused and bodily, to keep a watch out for someone else? On your relations, ask folks what they want help with and exactly what they do not require help with this; you can steer clear of over-venturing different folks' limits.

Enneagram 3

A three your annoyance for advancement, achievement, and a sense that you've achieved something important on the planet. You're especially objective arranged, and you also enjoy collecting grants and graphics of advancement because you experience life. Now you have an inclination which you ought to keep on accomplishing and accomplishing things together with the aim you will feel valuable instead of useless. You might have become lauded for your accomplishments yet feeling imperceptible when you were not achieving anything. You might have felt like in order to acquire your place in this world, you had to find the right home, the appropriate garments, a suitable vehicle, or possess the perfect job. There and here it really well might debilitate feeling this burden towards advancement. At the stage when you are rationally sound and adult, you will need generally action naturally certain, innovative, committed, and inspirational. At the stage when you are rationally juvenile or undesirable, you could be prideful, worn out, and materialistic.

What to Do:

Invest Some energy in mind analysing that which you achieve for YOU and everything you do to pursue success and the acceptance of others. Discover someone you can depend on to impart your vulnerabilities too. This is sometimes difficult in light of how you will need to appear cultivated and self-continuing yet much as might be anticipated. Notwithstanding, having a person who's sheltered, non-judgmental, and dependable to converse is important. Uncovering your real self to a person may seem to be unnerving, yet it will probably make you charming to this person rather than less. You will also develop a level of confidence and realness that is going to help you with feeling loved for who you are rather than what you're doing.

Enneagram 4

A Massive number feel as they are strange ducks in a universe teeming with traditionalists. They, for individual nature and noteworthiness, nevertheless feel as though it is ceaselessly beyond their own control. They often feel like other individuals, very similar to nobody can appreciate them see who they're. They're often creative and considerate, attracted to tales, craftsmanship, poetry, or music, which encapsulates a tendency they struggle to express keywords.

Ordinarily, Fours climbed up tendency not quite exactly like every other individual in their loved ones. They and then state this as feeling like a "vagrant" in their house because they had no one they can connect to or find comfort with. More than anything, Fours have to feel as though they have a place on this planet, some significance, to deliver their inner experience and personality out beyond any limiting influence.

What to Do:

Concentrate In your thoughts and start to observe whenever you have the urge tore up them." Here and there, you may feel disliked, disregarded, or misconstrued with no evidence to assist those thoughts. Get rude awakenings in the people you think when you believe you are being judged, scrutinized, or preserved a tactical distance from. Do whatever it takes to not "overinterpret" each movement and comment made concerning you. As a four, you want to get a one of a kind ability or experience, something which separates you. Once in a while, it will be hard to start, however. Placing the state of mind on your area or house can have a significant impact! Look at making an "atmosphere" in your area that advances motivation and imagination. Print out images that inspire you, establish a container with blossoms which cause you to feel silent, light a fire. Consider small ways in which you can get involved in dispositions of stability rather than disturbance.

Enneagram 5

A five, you want to view the way the world works, and you love investing a lot of energy in evaluation, study, and studying. You truly feel just like on the off probability which you are able to accommodate enough or have sufficient authority over 1 subject you will be fit and outfitted. However, it frequently feels as though your quest for advice is insufficient to meet you. You worry your aptitude is not helpful enough or does not make you proficient enough. You worry being defenceless, captured without satisfactory info, or overpowered. You may generally feel as if you need to collect life, uninterrupted time, distance to yourself, energy to yourself. Folks will generally fume you in large parts, and you often feel over-invigorated and stressed by their orders and interferences. You feel that a good need to possess ability in 1 area that will cause you to feel connected and capable on Earth.

What to Do:

Concentrate On when you are feeling subject so far as anyone is concerned. How does this make you feel on your own? Is it true that you're ignoring different elements of your life that require your thought? Self-care, companionships, health, and household relations are, for the large part, important. It has a tendency to be easy that you feel lost out of your own body – a "phone, speaking thoughts" of types. It's possible to start to dismiss your physical and societal demands, which only hurts you within the long haul. Try to enter your body or another.

Place in virtually no time daily journaling your physical and psychological experience. Try to commit some energy occupied using bodily motion such as exercising, jogging, bicycling, or hand to hand fighting. At the stage as soon as your body is wakeful, your mind is more honed, and you'll have more access to some emotional assets. You will also feel less frustrated and concentrated. Give coming at a snapshot to someone you care about daily. Irrespective of whether it is only a simple, immediate message or an email, these dependable endeavours in your part is going to aid you with a feeling associated with your overall environment.

Enneagram 6

As An enneagram six, you an annoyance to get a sense of experiencing a location and trust along with your overall environment. You often battle to think on your own decisions and decisions; you fear which you will settle in an inappropriate option, you'll confide in an improper person, or be left without anybody else unequipped for coping with what life tosses at you. You want to be organized, and you are exceptionally vital, considering alternative courses of action for every direst result possible that enters your own thoughts. You hope that you're able to be organized sufficient for whatever comes to your own leadership, and you also profoundly want network financing and safety -- a method of confidence and reliable convictions you may depend on. At the stage when life is silent and what's moving smoothly, you will generally sense on edge, trying to find items that you might have missed or possible catastrophes that could creep up on you. You will need this uneasiness to depart, yet you are so focused around profitability and willingness which you are able to eat out yourself.

What to Do:

Likely The best problem that Sixes have will be expecting to build security in their state without settling their very own passionate injuries or flaws. Try to journal about your anxieties, feelings of fear, and anxieties and following that pinpoint what's tripping them and what amount of having materialized. What would it resemble about the off possibility you could relinquish even 75 percent of those anxieties? What could be the possible additions or misfortunes? Have a stab at posting 10 items every day which made you feel safe or stable. Might you be able to focus on those zones more? Work on living in the time and relinquishing the pursuit of possible calamities. Work on being with yourself instead of always functioning and functioning up that safety that always seems to be remote. Grow some calm time for yourself every day with the aim which you're able to ease your mind. Go for strolls, workout, and join with your entire body. Doing so can push one to overeat and sense all the more logically participated and clear on your rationale.

Enneagram 7

You are among the most courageous, hazard taking personality types of the enneagram. You cherish travel and trying new things. It seems as though your mind is humming with ideas and options to explore. You profoundly desire the presence of energy, fun, and gratification. Your anxiety about passing up a fantastic chance, being tired, or refused of these valuable things during everyday life. You pursue opportunity and satisfaction, yet there and here it seems as though there is an inward tension which you are fleeing from within your search for pleasure and expertise. You might wind up consistently distracted, leaping from action to act instead of finishing the situations you begin.

What to Do:

Function On viewing your yearning for new items. Would you really feel like about the off possibility that you try another movement or get another thing which you will at this point be optimistic? Pause for a moment to find the magnificence and marvel in the minute you are as of today encounter. What bliss is readily accessible right since you likely won't discover as you continued searching for the brand new? At the stage when you are tired, focus on documenting your musings rather than locating another activity. What factors, recollections, or emotions is that exhaustion raising for you? Do some of these oughts to be handled rather than preserved a strategic space from? Work out how to listen out yourself along with your thoughts when you are tired instead of search after something different.

Enneagram 8

You are someone with a massive measure of resolve and energy. You endeavour to become solid and autonomous, and you've got confidence in being continuous and discomfort through almost any hardship. You long to get a sense of solidarity inside yourself, solidarity to safeguard yourself, and the ones that you despise. You require the opportunity to pick your specific way of life. You despise being commanded; basically, imagining that it makes you feel angry and baffled. The most important issue for this is today, and your quest for freedom can make you secure towards intimate relations, unfit to connect with folks, or become defenceless about them. You may also front of your fear of dismissal or humiliation by obstructing different people's jobs to port with you to a deep level. You need to put yourself out there could force you to lose your sense of control and chance.

What to Do:

If you are very similar to most eights, there was a period in your childhood when you had a sense you must be that the "experienced youth" in your loved ones. You needed to carry on a slew of duties, and you also had a sense you could not generally let off your gatekeeper or behave naturally. You did not harp in your pain. Instead, you opted to bring your life in your hands -- make sure yourself, protected those closest to you, and be adventurous and in-control. Whatever the case, something which could help you with recovery and find harmony is coping with your own distress and also the childhood which you might believe you did not get the opportunity to get. Explore some of the explanations for why you see yourself from jealousy -- what could happen on the off likelihood that you opened to someone or at the event you approached someone for aid? You do not have to go ahead and keep everything to anybody who may be in the area, nevertheless denying your damages may prompt sharpness, self-assurance, and outrage.

Enneagram 9

Agreeable and grounded from the normal Earth, you for external stability. You have to develop concordance on your overall environment, and you try to become patient and functional in everything that you do. As a Nine, your annoyance for inner amicability so unequivocally you risk dismissing clashes, obliging other people at any event, once you would prefer to not, or making light of the importance of issues during your lifetime. You might "look at" if there's strife inside yourself or in character around you.

You may generally subdue outrage, believing that if you happened to take part in the emptiness or state your dissatisfaction, you would lose that inward arrangement you need.

What to Do:

At whatever stage you are feeling "considering" of your surroundings, consider what place of your requirement to get this done. What danger did you really see? Can it be a Risk you need to manage? Which are the Pros and Cons of "looking at" instead of tuning in? Basically, contemplating these Things can help you with being mindful once you need to visit Bat for something or join instead of a draw. You may generally subdue Your own indignation, believing that it is not okay to express your requirements or requirements in case it might mess concordance. Discover that it is alright to be Furious once every so often. Work on disapproving of the Things Which You would like Not To perform. Inform yourself that folks will not instantly despise you or Reject you on the off probability that you simply go to bat on your own indeed, they can Respect you over the long haul.

Conclusion

The eight lead to conclusions and take action unexpectedly and decisively. Other humans may need a lot more time to look at the big picture and know what to do about it. Therefore, on which E eight takes initiative and drives, humans feel unprepared or overwhelmed.

Even though eight are working hard to preserve their vulnerability from other people, they can display it more than they realize, especially in moments of reflection or anticipating future challenges.

When people are unable to assert themselves or control themselves clumsily, the Sites will quickly take charge of situations. They assess that any person is susceptible, which may lead them to ignore what others are announcing or offering.

The eight do not react properly to being convicted through dishonesty or others.

Eight do not conform to the rules and hate any attempt at being controlled. At the same time, their tendency to take control assumes that others will follow and conform to them. This can cause anxiety in relationships.